A guide to successful retirement

Harry Austin

Working • Retiring • Reinventing • Thriving

Published by: WriterAuthor

ISBN 978-1-0686415-0-3 – Print
ISBN 978-1-0686415-1-0 - eBook

Edited by Suzanne Arnold
Cover Design by Ardel media Ltd.

www.writerauthor.co.uk

When you retire,
you don't expire.

CONTENTS

INTRODUCTION

This book brings together a collection of topics not considered by your financial adviser. It is not about your pension nest-egg or investments. Instead, this book guides you to see a successful retirement is one that will only be built around you, by you. A successful retirement is not one that is ready-made or indeed served to you by money. This book seeks to entertain, inform, and inspire your time in retirement.

We look at:
- The end of working life and what happens to us as we approach the big day.
- How to find our new routine, identity, and purpose.
- How the mind and body will age, and what we can do (and not do) to prolong a healthier retirement.
- How to prevent boredom and not be ambushed by alcohol and gambling.
- What you can do if money is tight.

For those that like to skim-read, each chapter starts with **a quick read** that summaries the chapter's key points.

Whatever your plans,
Whatever your dreams,
Each day the sun will rise,
And each day the sun will set,
What you do with this light is in your hands.

CHAPTER 1

THINKING ABOUT RETIREMENT

QUICK READ

When do we decide to retire?

The day of retirement is a significant life-marker. There will be reflections as you transition from a working life to one of leisure. And yet, there may be concerns about money. You ponder on what to do with your expanse of free time. You fear boredom. One solution to these anxieties is to liberate your thoughts away from the financial. Money is important, yes, but you also have a body and mind to care for too.

You have a strong duty to make the best of your time. Retirement is sustained by a healthy body, a cognitive mind, and money. Without a healthy body, we have no other to carry us. Without a sound mind, there is no place for thoughts. Without planning our money, we risk losing life experiences. The answer is to seek good health.

If there is one key to a successful retirement, that is to stop working when financially able. Older retirees often reflect upon this. They regret losing the optimal moment by continuing to work. With hindsight, in the last decade of life, they now value time more than money.

This book covers the fundamentals of this new chapter in your life. Starting from the last months of working life, to understanding the changes the mind and body will endure. Life (as long as we shall live) is to be enjoyed and embraced. Because now you have the money, you now have the time too.

(End of quick read)

THE DAWN OF RETIREMENT

Before 1909, our ancestors had little expectation of life after work. Working life was just that. They worked for life. There was no social care or state benefit. The phrase "state pension" hadn't even been invented yet. In 1909, the average life expectancy was below sixty years.

Reaching today's retirement age of sixty-seven was not the norm. It was common to find us in the graveyard at this age. But today, with a life expectancy much greater, many people reaching the age of sixty-seven have twenty years of leisure ahead of them.

The longest lived person is recorded as Jeanne Calment. Born in 1875, she passed away in August 1997, making her 122 years old. Although she is officially recognised as the oldest person, there are circulating doubts.

Sceptics claim it was Jeanne Calment's daughter who falsely held the record. They say she took her mother's identity to avoid inheritance tax. The oldest man on record is Jiroemon Kimura (1897–2013) who lived to the age of 116.

Few of us will reach that age. Sorry. In the western world, the average lifespan is eighty-two. Today's average life expectancy. If you retire in your early sixties, you may well hope to have another twenty years of life ahead. That said, with modern medicine and protection against diseases, one in five of us will still reach our hundredth birthday. One in a hundred will live beyond the centenarian milestone. Sadly, however, one in five of us will not reach retirement age.

But for most of us, today, retirement is not the end, but a new life stage. Therefore, today's retirement is a gift. The reward of healthy leisure time we receive after a lifetime of hard work. But little prepares you, or any of us, for retirement. There is no interview or readiness assessment. Financial advisers will steer us part of the way. They encourage us to build a nest-egg to ease concerns over money. Those who pay our pension have little interest in our wellbeing. Unless we are prepared, our retirement can become dull and directionless.

Your goal before and after retirement is therefore to find a new identity, a new purpose, and to maintain the best of health.

THOUGHTS OF RETIREMENT

Deciding when to retire is one of life's significant light-bulb moments. A moment when you have a range of reflections as you compare and reconcile your working life with the prospect of full-time leisure. You hope your pension is ready, but this isn't a time for impulse decisions.

To have a successful retirement needs planning. Not just the money aspect (which is not the subject of this book), but to foresee a retirement that has a purpose. A retirement that gives fulfilment, a new identity and a reason not to be isolated at home. But first, when do you retire?

Your age is but one benchmark to guide you. There are also influences at work, among friends and even the time of year. However, if there is one secret to a successful retirement, it is not to use the last two decades of good health just to work. Aim to retire before you expire.

First steps

Until a certain day, we are happy to exchange our youth, time, and energy for financial reward. But then one day, our thoughts of retirement are triggered. Perhaps a close friend tells you of their retirement plans, your partner retires, or the boss questions your worth on the payroll. Whatever the trigger, these thoughts of retirement will stay with you.

Slow wave trigger
For many people, one of the slow triggers is celebrating their fiftieth birthday and the arrival of their sixth decade. Prefixing our age with a 5 (instead of a 4) makes us reflect on life thus far. We question our life choices and seek new meaning and purpose. We believe our best years are now behind us, although, in truth, we are still fairly young. But as our metabolism slows, we gain weight all too easily. We find our energy levels dipping and, on the weekend, an afternoon nap is a pleasure. We ask, is it time to retire?

Another trigger might be thoughts surrounding our career. Some people feel they've reached the apex and there are few remaining challenges. Each year, advancing technologies are grabbing away our cherished skills. As a result, we feel less functional in the workplace. Our enthusiasm for learning new skills is lower, and we feel disconnected from our career. We ask, is it time to retire?

We learn about the deaths of those barely older than us. We see our own mortality when Mr. X dies at sixty. We hear the first tick of our life expectancy clock. Thinking life is too fragile, we ask, is it time to retire?

On this day, the slow wave triggers will help us connect the threads of our lives:
- With the mortgage mostly paid, you can lower your salary income.
- The children have become independent adults.

- Savings are healthy.
- Do you really want to work until you drop?
- Maybe you only need to work part-time.

Once we have these considerations aligned, we reconcile ourselves to the idea of replacing working days with life in retirement. Despite this, there remains anxiety about departing from work. We ask how long will our money last? What will we do with ourselves? Asking ourselves these questions is human nature. We fear the worst and remain working to ease the money anxiety.

There is little certainty in life. And while the uncertainty over retirement stays with us, we are reluctant to change the status quo. Fearing change, we put the success of retirement at risk. We risk delaying our departure from working life for too long. We can learn from the story of Mr. Newton who tells of his frustrations with being an older retiree:

"When I look back, I wish I hadn't worked into my late 60s. Time and health are much more important than money."

Snap trigger
There are also snap triggers that push us into making the retirement decision. The final straw that broke the back of working life, so to speak.
- Being disrespected by someone in authority.
- Having an extra stressful day.
- Finding ourselves unappreciated for working long or unpaid hours.
- Feeling a conflict brewing with a coworker.
- Hearing our spouse announce their retirement.

It is a defining, snap moment. But, should you retire at this moment? This is the subject of our next few sections;

we will also look at those moments when it makes sense to pause any thoughts of retirement.

Fear of change
Einstein once noted that shifting your viewpoint can transform what you perceive. Granted, retirement is a significant lifestyle change, but do think beyond the retirement challenge. Challenges such as:

- Anxiety over money.
- Loss of identity.
- Boredom and lack of purpose.
- Social isolation.

Later chapters will cover these subjects, but, for now, consider the advice you would give a friend. Because. we are better at giving advice than taking it. By listening to your internal voice, you can build a better retirement for yourself, your family, and your friends.

EXPLORING YOUR TRANSITION
When you're ready for retirement, it's time to plan the journey you'll take to achieve this milestone. There are two common approaches: the cliff-edge and the phased retirement.

Cliff-edge approach
The cliff-edge approach is mostly associated with the traditional retirement model. A model where you spend most of your working life paying into a pension, ultimately to provide a nest egg. And then, when you're ready, you drop your employee badge and take your nest egg into retirement. On the Friday your working life ends; on the Monday, an new lifestyle begins. Metaphorically, you have stepped over a cliff-edge into retirement.

With a fixed date, you have years of anticipation. You are excited and looking forward to your retirement day. When that Monday morning arrives, you have pension income and ample free time.

Those who favour the cliff-edge approach say:
- There is a line in the sand that gives clarity to retirement. The simplicity of knowing when our working life is expected to stop.
- With planning and best foresight, the cliff-edge approach can give us financial stability in later years.
- If we are prepared for retirement, the cliff-edge model will maximise retirement free time.

However, others argue that this approach is too extreme. You risk a vacuum forming between full-time working life and sudden full-time retirement.

The disadvantages are:
- An abrupt loss of purpose. You can feel isolated at home and find boredom.
- Income reduction will be swift. Plus, you lose the opportunity to increase income by working extra hours.
- Lower physical activity will affect your health.
- You may have trouble adjusting to retirement life. With a sudden expanse of free time, you may struggle unless you have hobbies and activities.

Jay, a new retiree, tells us:
"I was used to working long hours and sometimes too exhausted for housework and shopping. But, when I retired, housework and shopping were all I had. Bored and aimless, I contemplated going back to work."

Phased approach
A phased approach is where you transition into retirement gradually. Rather than shutting the door on

your working life at a specific date, you are eased into retirement by reducing your working hours. By working part-time, you keep hold of your purpose and daily structure. And yet, you create free time to build new routines and social circles outside the workplace.

There are benefits to a phased approach, for you and your employer:
- A gradual reduction in work-related stress eases you into the slow lane.
- You keep your sense of purpose and your social connections at work.
- Phasing smooths your financial dependence on employed income.
- Employers keep your skills and knowledge for longer. Until your full retirement, you could mentor younger workers.

You can approach phasing in one of two ways:
- Maintain your weekly workdays, but cut back on daily hours. For example, replacing the 9am to 5pm Monday to Friday with 9am to 1pm Monday to Friday.

- Work the same number of hours per day but reduce the number of days worked per week. For example, replacing the 9am to 5pm Monday to Friday with 9am to 5pm Monday to Wednesday.

With the first option, your coworkers will see you working shorter days. As you leave early, it can irk them as they remain at work. In some circumstances, resentment can build. With the second choice, you work the same hours each day as your coworkers.

The second choice is thought to work well. Reduce working days to three, giving you half a week to explore

A guide to successful retirement

hobbies and to expand your social networks.

While a phased approach is the best of both worlds, there are several disadvantages:

- It might disconnect you from new projects in the workplace. Isolation can build and your worth decline. You may feel deflated when not asked for input.
- Management must define your responsibilities to prevent tensions with coworkers.
- Feeling part of a team will fade. No longer full-time, you miss spontaneous social events. Coworkers may feel uneasy over your innocent exclusion.
- Working a reduced number of days (or hours) may not provide the same sense of accomplishment or fulfilment as working full time.
- It can be difficult for employers to manage and coordinate a phased retirement.

If you opt to take a phased approach, you must set expectations with upper management and coworkers. No one should expect you to squeeze a normal working week into a reduced number of hours. Or take work home (physically or mentally) to meet deadlines.

Meeting deadlines should be consigned to the past. If the company has agreed to reduced hours, they should make provision to accommodate this.

For the most part, deadlines are no longer your problem. Remember, you are in training for retirement.

And lastly, a phased retirement will also stop you from going from something to nothing.

FORCED RETIREMENT
Redundancy is a form of forced retirement. While the terms on offer can be tempting (to grab the cash and go) you are still being wholly punted into retirement. Failing health can also control your working life and force retirement. Either way, the change of lifestyle will be challenging. In a short time frame, you lose your identity and purpose. You can become isolated at home without knowing what to do with yourself. Although this is challenging, it is also a time to reinvent yourself. You may choose to explore a new career, follow your passion, or opt for full-time retirement.

STAYING ON LONGER THAN PLANNED
You have asked the company for early retirement, and they have agreed. But now they are asking you to stay for another year. What should you do?

The reason you retire is to have a life that you call your own. Therefore, when your employer asks, what has the greater pull? Loyalty to the company or taking the reward of retirement?

Taking care of yourself should be foremost in your mind. However, ask yourself these questions:
- Does my role give me the right work/life balance?
- What is my overall job satisfaction?
- Does staying another year have any advantages?
- Could I ask for added benefits?
- Do I need another year of stress?
- Would working for another year change my long-term retirement goals?
- Could I reduce my responsibilities?
- At the end of the year, what happens next? Is a replacement being sought for next year?

Which lifestyle has the greater importance to you? A working life or a retired life? Where do you want to devote your good health?

PICKING THE RIGHT TIME

When is the best time to retire? This is a good question. If we speak to long-term retirees, the age when they retired features highly. Now with an ageing body, many feel they spent their health and mobility on working too long.

What age?

Delayed retirement is a common regret. Older retirees look back to their working days and wish they had retired sooner. Especially when the money was right. But the fear of reducing funds kept them working.

Now reflecting with declining health, they seek time, not money, in their later years. More time to travel, to enjoy simple reflections on a warm summer's day, or to see grandchildren become adults. Working too hard and for too long is one of their biggest regrets. Doing the things they loved while having rude health should have taken the driving seat.

Nobody wishes for more work time. A thought that captures the essence of finding a work/retirement balance. Finding the right time to leave work behind is a balance between knowing how to spend your money (budgeting) and when you are in good health.

And yet, working into later life can also play some part in keeping us healthier and happier. So, if your career is also your passion, and you are healthy and bonny, then soldier on.

TIME OF YEAR
The time of year you retire has some relevance. You might not initially feel much preference over which season to retire in, but we often associate retirement with a long summer holiday. And we imagine holidays as warm. Ideal beach weather or time to be in the garden sunshine with a gin and tonic. Retiring into colder days, with shorter daylight, can jar this imagery.

However, leaving working life in the winter has some benefits:
- With increasing age, your resistance to viruses declines. By staying away from commuters and fellow workers, you reduce your exposure to colds and bugs.
- Having that extra time in bed during the cold, dark mornings may improve overall contentment.
- There is also some logical charm to choosing the end of the year. If you align retirement with the Christmas holiday break, you avoid the dreaded return to work on 2 January.

TIME OF TAX YEAR
Retiring at the start of the new tax year can be financially beneficial. The new tax year refreshes your personal tax-free allowances and tax bands. When each tax year begins, there is a clean tax-slate for the year ahead.

Consider this simple comparison:

31 March 20xx:
In the last tax month of the year, an employee has twelve months of accumulated income that has taken them into the higher rate tax band of 40%. Adding a golden handshake of £15,000 on top will be taxed at 40%, costing the employee £6,000 in tax.

Same bonus on 30 April 20xx:
At the start of the new tax year, with only one month's salary, the accumulated income is still within the lower-rate tax band of 20%. A golden handshake of £15,000 will now be taxed at 20%, costing the employee £3,000 in tax.

A simple one-month delay will be saving the employee £3,000 in tax.

The UK tax year runs from the 6 April to the following 5 April. Please don't ask why! USA, 1 January to 31 December, Australia 1 July to 30 June. However, whatever the tax year is, it's every taxpayer's duty to arrange their affairs to save tax. This is known as tax avoidance, which is legal. The above is an example of tax avoidance by arranging one's affairs to save tax. On the contrary, tax evasion is not legal. Doing that would invite fines and jail time. And nobody should want to spend their retirement in jail.

Tax planning is a vast subject and very personal. To explore the tax landscape, talk to the professionals first. As their advice will come at a modest cost, there needs to be an element of economic judgement.

WHEN TO RETHINK
As we saw earlier, a snap moment can push you into a retirement frame of mind. But would it be the right moment to retire? Do you need to pause and rethink? As we will see shortly, a workaholic planning retirement will need to pause their plans.

Other common reasons to pause are:
Money
- Retirement income will not cover basic living expenses.

- Current debt is high.
- Struggling to pay historical bills.
- A major expense is on the horizon, but you have low funds to pay.
- Just hate working.

Social
- Only a few friends outside the workplace.
- Most social interactions are inside the workplace.
- Believing work is more important than social life.
- Thinking about work during holidays and weekends.

Feeling unprepared
- No idea how to spend the extra free time.
- Work gives you something to do.

If work holds a strong identification for you, leaving it behind may not be easy. This is the hard plight of the workaholic and those who experience burnout.

THE WORKAHOLIC: PLAN CAREFULLY

A workaholic will have a strong identification with their work and workplace. They work hard and use many hours to meet self-imposed deadlines. They need a challenge to find a purpose and to feel valued in the workplace.

To meet the challenge, social life takes a back seat. Times when they should be with their spouse, children, and friends. Despite the risk of these relationships turning sour, the workplace is where the workaholic wants to be.

The four common traits of a workaholic are:
- Taking work home (without reason).
- Checking for work messages when at home or on holiday.
- Trade personal relationships for work.
- Being reluctant to disengage from work.

A guide to successful retirement

When deep-rooted identity and purpose are found in the workplace, the workaholic will find it hard to leave. They may announce their retirement date but feel a powerful compulsion to stay.

If you identify with these traits, you need to break the work compulsion before the day of retirement. There is a fine balance to be found between work and leisure. But find it you must.

Time zones
The initial step involves dividing the day into two time zones. Create separate zones for work and home. For example:

Working life - 8am to 6pm.
Home life - 6pm to 8am.

Next, reduce the amount of work you take home, and then stop. Even if it means missing a deadline. Remember, you are now in training for retirement. The biggest shift in daily life. A time will come when you need to disconnect from work completely.

Messages
Stop checking for work emails at home. In fact, remove the ability entirely. The urge to check will be strong and unyielding at first, but breaking this habit will smooth your transition into retirement. It takes willpower and understanding of the challenge involved. It can take around ten weeks for a new habit to become automatic.

Holidays
When on holiday, assign a deputy to step in. Offer them training and create working procedures for them to follow. Set an auto-email rule to have all emails copied to them. And another to auto-move that email to a special

folder called "on holiday". This removes the feeling of being overwhelmed with unread emails when you return.

Ask not to be contacted while you are away. If there are any emergencies, the deputy should ask someone in higher authority first.

If you are that higher authority, trust the people below you to cope. They may even enjoy the challenge and appreciate your trust.

The aim here is to remove the deep-rooted habits of a career. Ready to experience a slower way of life. By disconnecting beforehand, you are gently breaking the habits. By slowing working life down, you are removing the ingrained routines that define your day. At first, you may feel a sense of loss with fewer work-related goals and deadlines. However, in time, you will find activities that redefine your goals and purpose.

Burnout
Burnout is when we are both physically and mentally exhausted. Working long hours under stress will often feature.

We may experience burnout because of:
- Feeling overwhelmed by work.
- Lack of control over work schedules (too many deadlines).
- Lack of support from management.
- Lack of recognition or reward.
- Lack of work/life balance.
- Poor communication and working relationships.
- Unclear job expectations or goals.

How long burnout lasts can vary from person to person. Some recover after a few days, whereas for others it becomes chronic and lasts longer. Burnout may persist for months (or even years) if it is not addressed.

The severity of burnout also varies. For some, the symptoms will be mild. For others, it can be so severe that it will affect the quality of life. Even into retirement.

Having the sensations of burnout just before retirement can be challenging. You can address things before the last day:
- Find a work/life balance to take care of physical and mental health.
- Set boundaries with your employer.
- Take full use of your holiday allowance.
- Practise self-care.
- Seek support from management.

Self-care is key. You may feel your work is all-important, but self-care will promote good health and give you a successful retirement.

LIFE PARTNER MATTERS
Although your retirement plans are personal, you should include your partner at an early stage. Share your vision and your perspective on the first year. Talk about your aspirations and the mundane, including:
- The transition.
- Changes to the daily routine.
- Home life.
- Holidays and travel.

How we divide household chores is an important part of home life. Without a conversation, you and your partner could be making different assumptions. If one partner believes they do more, harmony can be tested. According to the British Social Attitudes survey, Sixty-three per cent of women believe they carry a greater burden.

MARY'S STORY
When her husband David retired at sixty-two, Mary was in her late forties. Both had the funds ready to retire, but Mary loved her work. Retirement was enjoyable for David, but Mary's to-do list bothered him.

David's view: It was his time to relax. There was no rush to do anything, including Mary's list. He still did his share of domestic chores, so why was Mary getting annoyed?

Mary's view: What does he do all day? David ignores my to-do list, and I am still expected to do my usual share of housework when I come home.

Without having the right conversation, we risk making the wrong assumptions. Mary's to-do list has a greater urgency in her mind. Harmony in the household is breaking down.

The golden secrets are:
- Do not hold on to grudges over having to do more. Or what you perceive as doing more.
- Avoid complaining about what your partner fails to do. But appreciate what they do without prompt.

Second to retire
When the second partner retires, tensions may bubble in the home. The first will have established daily routines and found comfort in the quieter times. Disturbing these routines and creating noise may cause friction.

Joint retirement
Joint retirement is the perfect way to start a retired life. After decades of being apart during the day, you can

A guide to successful retirement

finally share your dream time together. Exploring activities, travelling, and looking after the grandchildren. Err... was that the plan?

Despite this, you must still plan daily life:
- How do you divide the household chores?
- Which activities do you share?
- Which activities do you pursue alone?
- Who looks after the money?
- Who will return to work if money becomes tight?

However, any joint retirement can have a darker side. Spending more time together. Over the years, we all change. When some people arrive at retirement life, they find their partner is no longer the person they fell in love with all those years ago.

A 2001 study found couples experienced more conflicts when they spent more time together during the day. Any irritations that existed before retirement are still going to be there. Now, they will be even louder and harder to ignore. There is no quick solution here. Be prepared to adjust and accommodate your partner's needs.

Over time, couples will settle into personal quiet zones. One morning, you are reading while your partner is tending the garden. Or, you may be near each other, but consumed by different passions. Psychologists call this parallel play. We have the comfort of being together, but not dependent upon the other.

CHAPTER 2

YOU HAVE DECIDED

QUICK READ

What control do you have over your retirement terms? If
they are controlled by external forces, you could leave
working life into disappointment. Having control can give
you a sense of empowerment, making retirement less
stressful. Will your employer agree to your plans? The
type of relationship you have with them is important.

If asked, are you ready to train and mentor your
replacement? It is a defining moment when you pass
down your years of wisdom. And yet, you may discover
what you know is now outdated. Newer processes are
being used by the younger generation.

As the last week approaches, the workplace will change. You feel there are some who are treating you differently. There are those who have already consigned you to the past. It would seem, you are becoming dispensable, even. Your forthcoming departure is changing the workplace dynamics.

And then, in the last week, you enter the waiting room. The waiting room marks both the end and a new beginning. The end of the familiar and the beginning of a new chapter. The third age. After decades of work, your days of freedom are finally here.

(End of quick read)

MASTER YOUR CONTROL

The more say you have about your retirement transition, the more fulfilling your retirement life will be. The more say you have, the more you can control your retirement wishes. Control is key.

Retirement planning will have two spheres of control. The internal locus of control and the external.

Internal locus

The extent of your control over events is defined by your internal locus of control. You decide and direct these events and moreover results which gives you a sense of empowerment. It is also self-motivating.

Having control over your retirement plans means you are less likely to be stressed. Stressed from the feelings of helplessness and from a forced transition. With control, you can build the perfect transition. Shape life after work with your input.

In short, control enables informed decision-making. Should events knock you back, you will be stronger and resilient. With self-belief, you will rebound and take the right steps. However, too much internal locus of control has drawbacks. If you make too many wrong decisions, you may feel overwhelmed. You are more likely to take the blame for all negative outcomes.

External locus

An external locus of control is where we think outside forces control our life and events. For example, luck, other people, or even divine influence.

We could even suggest there has been control over us throughout our lives.
- From birth to our late teens, our parents and

schooling directed us. We are told what to study, when to take exams, and prepare ourselves for the workplace.

- For the next 40 years, we park aside our internal locus of control for employment. While we have partial control, we are still time-restricted when trying to follow our passions. Earning a wage is a strong necessity.

Retirement grants us complete control for the first time. The freedom to do what we want. Retirement equals freedom.

RETIREMENT CONTROL

Not so long ago, retirement was forced upon us by the Default Retirement Act. This Act (now repealed) required all workers to leave the workforce at the state retirement age. Regardless of our own wishes, on reaching a certain age the work-barrier came down. The Act required us to transition into retirement. As it was wholly compulsory, employers had no choice but to request our departure.

This is an example of external control. As we approached our retirement birthday:

- We had little choice over our retirement planning.
- We were less likely to make reasoned decisions.
- With lower personal control, we had low engagement.
- We were less prepared for challenges or opportunities.
- We had less motivation to plan.

The dream of retirement became a nightmare for many. However, many businesses were in favour of this act. It was easier to plan their labour needs. It stopped less acceptable methods of removing older employees. And it created space for the younger generation.

And yet, through today's eyes, this act seems very harsh. But it was the legal framework around which the government paid the state pension. Our working life was a long countdown to a prescribed birthday. We had no control over when we retired. Life outside work had no gentle start with this cliff-edge act.

Thankfully, following a campaign by Age UK, the government abolished the Default Retirement Act in 2011. From this time, we could receive our state pension and continue with paid work.

THE EMPLOYER

If you are not employed, but have your own business to sell, see chapter 10 alongside this chapter.

With our retirement plan in hand, we approach our employer. This is where your plan may unwind, because the success of your plan hinges on two factors - the company's adhesion to the staff manual, and the relationship you have with your employer.

The relationship you have with your employer may be transactional or fair reward. Or shades between the two. To illustrate the idea, here is Ken's story:

For fifteen years, Ken had served his employer well. He did so with high skill and loyalty. Frequently, he had gone beyond his obligations. He was a true company person.

Thus, hoping to retire early with a reduced pension, Ken had expected his employer to be ready and willing to agree to his wishes. In his mind, this was the company's chance to reward him. But this is where Ken's retirement plans stumbled. The company refused Ken's request.

Why was this?

In Ken's case, the relationship he had with the company was transactional.

Transactional relationships

While the company thanked Ken for his loyalty, in their eyes, he was just doing his job. And in return, he received his contractual pay. With harsh rationality, they paid him to do a job. There are no other benefits or concessions. Plus, the company must treat every employee equally and adhere to the staff manual. We are sorry, Ken, but we must deny your request.

Fair reward relationship

Fair reward would have given Ken a different outcome. This is where the company shows appreciation and recognises his value. The company has seen Ken working hard and is sorry to see him go. They embrace Ken's retirement plans as their chance to reward him, and to say thank you. They even throw a surprise retirement party and give him a two-week cruise around the Mediterranean.

Negotiating

What if the company denies your retirement plans?

Begin by asking for an informal meeting. While you wait, read the staff manual and your employment contract. Look for terms relating to employee retirement. Next, note down what you see as a favourable outcome. Doing so will help you focus and avoid making bad concessions.

In the meeting, think of negotiating as a game of ping-pong. The ball represents the terms you hope to agree.

All parties will bat the ball across the table, trying to control the terms. Your role is to be flexible and keep the ball - your internal locus of control.

Control will flow between you and the company. If the company has too much control, stay focused on your ideal terms. Actively listen and empathise with the company. As they speak, repeat the words silently in your head. This will help you understand their needs. It will also build trust and rapport.
  - To avoid mistakes, be clear with suggestions.
  - Ask open-ended questions. This will help them put their viewpoint.
  - Can you be creative with solutions?
  - Be resilient if the negotiations become difficult.

If the negotiations stall, move the meeting forward with a minor concession. This is what psychologists call a "foot in the door".

It takes time and effort on your part to secure the retirement you want. However, disappointment is always a possibility. If you cannot agree, stand firm, walk away, and regroup.

There is always the option to resign. But that may affect your pension. Seek advice.

CULTIVATING THE SUCCESSOR

The company has agreed to your retirement plans, and the magical date is on the calendar. Your journey to retirement has begun. How you handover your role will define and conclude your employment journey.

The handover will fill you with mixed emotions. You are happy to retire, and yet there is a veneer of loss. Your lifetime of work is ending. You take pride in your accomplishments. But now you are ready to pass down your years of knowledge and insight. You are ready to become a trainer. You are happy to accept as a parting gift to the company.

Training

It is possible that nobody else knows how to perform your role. Not even management. If this is the case, do you want to leverage it when negotiating retirement terms? That said, training another can be both productive and rewarding. Be supportive as they learn and develop their skills. Training may test your patience at times.

Successful training requires clear goals and a positive attitude from both you and the trainee. Therefore, be open to what you see as silly questions. It is normal for the pace of learning to be slow. Your insight and perceptions are far greater than theirs.

Avoid dismissing any concerns. And be receptive to new ways of working. All industries change over time with new procedures developing. The trainee may tweak your methods to reflect current trends.

Mentoring

There are three elements to successful mentoring:

First, the **teaching element**. How you show the nuances of the work and what the company expects from them. Keep in mind that we all have different learning styles. Some prefer verbal instructions, while others like to work with manuals.

Next, the **supporting element**. As they make mistakes, offer corrective help and reviews. Making errors is part of their learning process. Making the same error twice, though, is a red flag.

And lastly, step back and **allow them to explore** without support, but be nearby to encourage and praise.

If they are repeating mistakes, or lack confidence, inform the company. While you may have concerns over their performance, aim to be detached from the ultimate responsibility. After your last day, you retire and leave the workplace. The trainee does not. If the trainee is not ready, the company must address the issue.

Company support
It would be unfair if the company did not support you during the training phase. They can help by:
- Managing a needs assessment to see what knowledge is needed before training starts.
- Paying for external courses, including the cost of travel to training events.
- Allowing you time to train.
- Providing training materials and tools, whether in print or online.

ENTER THE WAITING ROOM
After announcing your retirement, you slowly start to disengage from work. As you disengage, your colleagues will disconnect from you, too. Not purposely ignoring or avoiding you. But work projects and challenges are forever present. Any work-related debates, new projects, or decisions stay with the post-retirement team. Sorry to say, in their eyes, you are no longer there for the long term. It would be rare, however, for anybody to give you the cold shoulder.

Changing relationships with colleagues
As you near retirement day, the tone of conversation with colleagues will change. Reactions to your pending departure will differ. Some coworkers are happy for you

and share your excitement. Some are sorry to see you go. After all, they really like you. But others will worry. They are concerned about how it will affect them or the team. For them, the future looks uncertain.

You can guide their concerns by talking openly. Say what your leaving plans are and how you can help them today. It may just be a misunderstanding. Be kind-hearted and acknowledge their thoughts. Your departure is a change, and everyone will manage change differently.

An unhappy coworker can make leaving working life a challenge. However, you are not likely to change your plans because of them. But:

- Allow them to express their feelings and listen to their concerns. Try not to be defensive but understand their perspective.
- Ask management to offer a solution if they are worried about your retirement.
- Be open and honest about your reasons for retirement. Encourage them to share their thoughts and feelings.
- Offer solutions to their concerns. If they fear being left without your support, would they like training to upgrade their skills?

You may not change a coworker's perceptions, but listening and understanding can help you until the ultimate day.

The last week
Now in your last working week, you are tying up loose ends. You are clearing your workspace and, with a sense of anticipation, writing your special farewell message. Worldwide, this is a custom observed and enjoyed by 167,000 people every month.

And then you enter the waiting room.

The waiting room is a unique (once in a lifetime) mental space where you prepare for the transition into retirement. It is where you and your coworkers wait for the moment of farewell. The waiting room marks the end of one chapter, and a new beginning. The beginning of the third age.

THE LAST DAY

Your last day is another unique experience. Probably never to be repeated.

It will be a reflective moment in life to celebrate, but you will mourn the loss of your familiar world. As you recount the past, expect some emotional dips. For you, this is a momentous day.

The last day carries a ceremonial atmosphere. We hand over keys and reveal passwords that our boss did not know about. We stash away stationery for a rainy day. We are now ready to say our last words of goodbye.

Saying goodbye (a contraction of "god be with ye") will give rise to a few emotions. With pride, we feel a sense of satisfaction with our work. Our voice trembles as we thank those who gave their support and friendship. Most of our fellow workers will help us celebrate, with a promise to keep in touch.

IF YOU FEEL SPURNED

While the day is your special day, there may be those who have no interest. You note their name is not on the "Happy Retirement" card. Your coworkers will pause work to raise a glass in celebration, but those who spurn us stay working.

They give little importance to what is our special day.

This is not personal. There will be some with whom you have never connected. You know in advance they will not join the party. But some who spurn will concern us. There are those who experience a sense of loss when we leave the workplace. There are even coworkers who see our departure as betrayal.

Other reasons may include:
- A coworker relies on your support. Uncertain of how to manage without you, they fear losing their job.
- Your retirement may cause a meaningful change in the team dynamics. This can be unwanted or a hard change for some people.
- There is resentment and jealousy.
- Some people just dislike each other.

Remember
Avoid using the last day to exact revenge. The last chance to settle an old feud. You may relish the idea of telling John in accounts exactly what you think of him, but it will be a bad idea. He does not care for you either, and nothing positive will come if he fights back. A verbal boxing match is bound to sour the day and follow you into retirement. The memory of the final conflict will outlast the brief argument with John. Just say goodbye calmly. Offer some kind words and silently celebrate not crossing paths again. Wish them well and move on.

LETTING GO
One of the sobering thoughts is the realisation that our role and cherished workplace will move on without us. This day is part of the transition. From something familiar to something new. Familiar faces will become part of your history and not your destiny.

Knowing that our work friends will become part of our past is one of the retirement challenges. A few will miss us for a while. But over time, they too will change jobs, retire, or move away. The workplace community that we once thought was eternal will lose its durability and ebb away.

Scenario: Some years later, we bump into an old colleague. We learn Mouhib changed jobs not long after, Mike and Max set up a rival business. Vicky went to start a family and Barry, the star manager, retired. None of our old team remains. The significance of saying goodbye today will not be appreciated until later. Aspects of our working life will be missed (which is the subject of our next chapter). Our retirement day will be a cherished memory in the coming years.

CHAPTER 3

THE LEGACY OF WORK

QUICK READ

What are you leaving behind?

While on the day of retirement you gain your freedom from working life, you also leave behind a large part of your daily routine. A routine that is rooted in the workplace. Without knowing what is about to happen, you find the familiar daily life becoming part of your past. Is there anything you will miss about the workplace and this daily routine? Will it be your coworkers, the work, or the social side?

After leaving the workplace and your work friends, you risk finding a time-rich void. Unless you are prepared in advance to counter this void, you can move from something to nothing. Nothing is the act of doing little.

And avoiding nothing is one of retirement's biggest challenges.

Another challenge is to rediscover yourself. Not in the sense of meditating or finding a mountain guru. But, asking yourself who am I? Your work and workplace identity gave you elements of daily life that will disappear when you retire. This includes moments when people praise you and golden times when you achieve success.

Therefore, as you bid farewell to your working life, you must find a new, everyday purpose and identity.

(End of quick read)

LOST ESSENCE OF THE WORKPLACE

When leaving the waiting room, a door closes behind you, signifying the end of working life. Both physically and metaphorically. This physical door belongs to your workplace. And while you close that door for perhaps the last time, what are you leaving behind?

Dictionaries will define the workplace as "a place where people work". A more fitting badge could be: Uniting with others for a common cause. This is a better definition. However, this still focuses on the place rather than what it means for you.

The workplace can be how you define yourself. For many years, it has been the place where you held your identity. Where you understood your purpose. Although the workplace has a variety of roles and responsibilities, you enter the workplace (with others) to achieve a common purpose.

However, each morning as you enter the workplace, you may not give much thought to your two fields of life. You have a life inside the workplace and another outside. But the space inside, and coworkers around you, become part of your daily routine. Inside and outside merge into one seamless routine.

Life inside the workplace meets several important needs. Once retired we must replicate these needs with activities and hobbies.

The workplace holds:
- Our status, purpose, and identity.
- A predictable daily structure.
- Familiar faces and characters.
- Easy friendship and connections with others.

Therefore, as you leave the waiting room and close that door for the last time, all these things will go. Your life inside and outside the workplace will divide. Life inside the workplace will become part of your history. Meeting these needs is now reliant on life outside the workplace.

COWORKERS

A workplace is an excellent space for social interaction.

Inside the workplace, we find it easy to meet new friends and share rituals. We celebrate birthdays and personal news. For the most part, our bonding together is natural. And being natural, we have a degree of social intimacy. As a result, we enjoy belonging to the social group.

Friendships between coworkers inspire us to be supportive. Be willing to help the wider social group. So much so that businesses encourage us to be supportive by developing team spirit with play. By introducing play, they bring a brief pause to the working day. A time to relax and have some fun.

Work-play encourages us to be social. By engaging with coworkers, we build camaraderie within the workplace. Play-time helps us share common values, too. The more social interactions and shared common values, the greater our engagement with the company. We know this engagement as the team spirit, and it can empower us to perform our best and stay engaged with our work.

This part of daily life will leave us the day we retire. The familiar social circle will fade after our last day. This is why some find leaving working life behind too hard. Retirement introduces the fear of being lonely.

To prevent loneliness and isolation, those who fear retirement stay working. For them, each workday is a chance to escape a lonely life. Earning a wage has a lower meaning. They may even not enjoy their work, but a life without work puts them at risk of boredom, isolation, and depression. Losing the workplace life is an enormous concern to them.

LOSING THE ACTIVE CAREER JOURNEY

From the day we join the workforce to the day of retirement, there are five working life phases. These generally follow each other in logical order. But the boundaries between each are hard to define.

The working life phases are:
- At twenty, we adopt a career and engage.
- Passing the age of thirty, our career is developing well. We explore the opportunities.
- Now forty, we are approaching a career apex.
- In our fifties, working life is changing. Our career engagement declines.
- At sixty we disengage, with thoughts of retirement.

However, there is some evidence to suggest that reaching the milestone age of fifty causes many to reconcile retirement with mortality. Fifty is when we ponder life beyond work. We know no one will live forever. Not yet anyway. At fifty, we are still healthy and mentally sharp. Feeling life is too short, we crave adventures before we pass away.

At the dawn of our sixtieth birthday, we recall events from twenty years ago. They seem like yesterday. We sense time is speeding up as each year passes. All too soon, we are halfway to seventy.

When does one's working life end? Do we see a life outside of work and then detach from our careers? Or do we disengage from our career and then decide to retire? The evidence is not that conclusive. However, whatever the true reason, age research is encouraging. At sixty, we can hope for another twenty years of life. And we might enjoy good health for most of these years.

HAVE SOMETHING TO LOOK FORWARD TO

Retirement can cause us to enter a space of nothingness. Unprepared, we go from something - work - to nothing. After working life, retirement creates a void. And to stop this, one of your retirement challenges is to go from something (when you leave behind your work life identity and status) to something (new daily routines, a new purpose and a wider social life).

If you do not prepare for your new time-rich lifestyle, there is a risk of going from something to nothing. And while nothing may sound dreamy, after the honeymoon period has faded, having nothing to do will turn sour. Knowing this is one of your keys to a successful and happy retirement.

Be prepared

As the workplace door closes behind you, be prepared to let go. Let go of your career and the significance the workplace has played. A time will come when these two things and workplace friends will not be part of daily life. In retirement, work-life is the life you are leaving behind.

Even before entering the waiting room, be ready to create a new meaning and purpose for retirement life. You can achieve this by finding fresh activities and hobbies. Now you are free from the shackles of working life, you become time-rich to explore new endeavours.

As new life in the third age unfolds, think about past ambitions. Create a new daily structure and remember the importance of exercise. Allocate some of your fresh time to foster connections with family and friends, new and old.

Being prepared and doing these things will avert a boring, aimless, and depressive retirement life. New retirees who are unprepared feel life has no purpose. For them, the only resolution is going back to work.

THINGS YOU MAY MISS

A lifetime of work goes beyond a regular income. There are intangible aspects to our working life. And they go unseen or unappreciated until we leave working life. These aspects fortify life and how we connect with others:

- Status.
- Identity.
- Appraisal.
- Flow.
- Golden moments.

Status

Over the course of your career, you have gained a level of ability in the workplace. You have earned this respected ability through years of experience, performance, and reputation. Status and authority come from these. You may have tied your work title to your status. A title that stakes your place in the chain of command. The presence we have in the workplace. For those of us with a high status, you may even enjoy special privileges both inside and outside the workplace.

Leaving a working life means you leave this status behind. When the workplace door closes, you must leave behind your rank and hierarchical thinking. Thus, retiring often brings the challenge of losing status.

A guide to successful retirement

Until retirement, many of us use status to measure our worth. A measure taken from the contribution we made to the workplace. All this, our status and self-perceived authority, will become part of our past life. As we leave, our status and authority are handed over to the next generation. This does not mean our achievements are diminished. We have made our contribution.

Identity
Your workplace identity has been part of life for forty years. You may have said "I'm an accountant", but now this is changing. As you enter retirement, your identity (given by your career and what you wear) will fade. On the day of retirement, you will lose your workplace identity. The ready-made title of accountant no longer applies. Some find the absence of identity challenging. For others, the loss is liberating. But the question still remains. Who are you now?

Many of us will change our identity by saying, "I'm a retired accountant." There is little wrong with wearing any retirement badge. It gives a frame of reference for those who ask. However, does this accurately reflect your identity?

Your new identity will grow slowly. With the abundance of free time, you can revisit past hobbies or seek new passions. You will follow your personal ambitions. As working life fades, you will lose the persona of work. Instead, you look for comfort and personal expression.

Appraisal
During our working life, we may become accustomed to being thanked and appreciated. When we are, we feel motivated to do our best. Our sense of worth, morale, and pride increase. As a result, we become engaged with our work. Being told we are contributing meaningfully

is rewarding. Positive appraisal makes us happy. Initially, our moments of appraisal will decline after working life.

Flow
Flow is a state of mind. A state when we become so immersed in a task that our deep engagement gives us a sense of joy and satisfaction. By applying our skill and ability, we achieve flow. During flow, we find our thoughts and actions are free from distractions. We are "in the zone". Time will fly by. Flow ignites our brain's reward pathways. Having flow pushes aside daily stress.

We can experience flow from our work. And when flow arrives, we are no longer reliant on the outcome for reward. Instead, the reward is from the engagement. When we combine engagement with the desire to reach perfection, we enter flow.

It is time to seek a different flow in retirement. Seek opportunities to develop skills with clear goals. Take part in new hobbies and activities. Not only will we find new meaning and purpose beyond working life but also general happiness and satisfaction. If we do not, there is a risk of low motivation and becoming aimless.

Golden moments
Golden moments are times of fulfilment. Times when we complete a special project or solve a difficult problem. In working life, they bring enjoyment and stand out as special times. These are golden moments that remind us why we love doing what we do.

Reaching these moments in retirement may be harder. However, if we embrace the new, and cultivate new experiences, we can find our golden moments again. Discover purpose in this new life chapter. Even if it means stepping outside your comfort zone.

A guide to successful retirement

CHAPTER 4

THE CHALLENGES

QUICK READ

What to do now.

The first retirement day may feel strange. You are at home on a workday. No parking issues or battles with a crowded commuter train. Today marks the beginning of a time-rich life. What will you do when you have an entire day to yourself?

At first, we are drawn towards the act of doing nothing. A time when doing nothing (or at least doing very little) aligns with our early thoughts about retirement. This is a time we call the honeymoon period. However, there will come a time when daily inactivity no longer feels like retirement bliss. Too much idleness will become stressful.

When retirement becomes lonely, boring, and aimless, it is time to build new routines for the week. Having a structure helps manage the extra time we have in retirement. A successful retirement needs a new long-term purpose. A purpose that is supported by your values and which gives meaning to retirement life.

Being social is all part of our happiness. Our social interactions are a lifelong human need that becomes more important as we enter the third age. The shift away from the workplace to a more solitary existence can pose challenges.

We can be social and be connected by using technology. However, if we have opted out of change, it is less easy. While changes can be daunting, we should be proactive towards learning. The smartphone is a good example. Instant communication and connection to health-monitoring devices. Technology becomes a bridge to the growing world.

(End of quick read)

DISCOVER FRESH PURPOSE

Previously, we spoke about flow, status, and identity. And yet, while we have explored these, there is still little that prepares us for full-time retirement. Having a purpose in full-time retirement is decisive.

If we reflect on the past forty years, your career has given you a purpose. If you were an engineer, for example, your purpose was to design and build bridges, hospitals, and shopping centres. And thus, you made a contribution to something much larger than yourself. A career as an engineer sustained a long-term purpose. That purpose gave you values and meaning in your daily actions. In other words, thus far, you have led a meaningful life.

Having a meaning is at the heart of our lives. Without a meaning (to life), we become aimless, idle, and lack emotional wellbeing. Therefore, as you leave working life, you must find a new purpose that provides meaning and value. This is difficult when your career has given you purpose with little effort on your part. But we all need a purpose, plus value, to equal our meaning. We need to retire from something (work) to something (as yet unknown).

FINDING NEW PURPOSE

In the first year of retirement, we gravitate towards external sources to find our new purpose. We travel, play golf, or watch the world go by. We also volunteer or even engage with activities just to keep busy. In the first year of retirement, we are happy. In our time-rich world, these things are fresh adventures.

But these adventures will only give us a short-term purpose. Over time, we tire of playing golf or travelling. What was once entertaining has now become boring.

When this happens (and it will), we feel less satisfied with the substance of our new activities. To fix this, we seek another external source. And so, the cycle begins.

The key is to find a long-term purpose. One that connects to your passions and aspirations. What to suggest is flavoured by your preferences and can take on various forms.

But to give an idea:
- Continuous personal growth and learning
- Campaigning for social justice
- Living sustainably.

You can allow the purpose to find you. Metaphorically. You have nobody to please, no deadline to meet. Finding a new purpose is almost an ambling process. You may find it when you're not expecting to.

FINDING YOUR VALUES
We all have core values. They help us steer our place in the world and how we behave with others. Often, they are deeply personal. They guide our integrity, loyalty, and sense of fairness. We believe in and strive to uphold these principles (and more).

Looking deeper into the human psyche, we can connect a series of personal nuances:
- Our thoughts...will be our words.
- Our words...will be our actions.
- Our actions...will be our habits.
- Our habits...will be our values.
- Our values...will guide us.

Society values
These are the values we adopt and hold by seeing the social behaviour around us. We are expected to exhibit

these behaviours as well.
- Act with honesty, integrity, and intention.
- Accept responsibility for our thoughts and behaviour.
- Respect others.
- Have compassion and humour.
- Have ambition and drive.
- Think of others before ourselves.

We know these values as global values. They are not unique to any one person. It is how our society functions.

Inherited values
Inherited values, however, are from our family. Anchored from a youthful age, they often become our core values. When we see our mother as artistic, for example, we attach a value to creativity in adult life.

Intuitive values
We gather our intuitive values from curiosity, courage, and tenacity. They are not values that we conclude from intellectual thought. They are instinctive. We sense danger without supporting logic. We have a gut feeling about... To the world at large, your values are the cornerstone of your character.

LINK TO MEANING
With the understanding of purpose, and an appreciation of values, we can join the two to see a bigger picture.

Our meaning.
- With a long-term purpose, you will have a sense of direction and clarity.
- Holding values guides you to what is important and worthwhile. Values will enhance the chosen purpose.

FINDING MEANING

To find meaning from an activity, we combine our purpose and values. When the activity has ended, the flavour of the activity, and the experience we enjoy, will stay with us. Take a simple example of painting a picture.

The value we extract from painting a picture is the value of being artistic. The purpose is to see, absorb, and enjoy the mindfulness we experience from the act of painting. The meaning is the completed picture. We are proud of our painting. We receive creative recognition, and the memory of the activity will linger on.

Dr Henry Cloud, respected for his clinical psychology, says only ten per cent of our happiness comes from where we are mindfully present. The other ninety per cent comes from our thoughts. In other words, ninety per cent of our happiness lives in the mind. Our purpose and value lives in the mind. This is why money will not make us happy in the long term.

We can also link meaning to our experiences. Experiences that give us a sense of accomplishment and help us feel more connected to the world.

YOUR FIRST DAY

Celebrate this first day. The arrival of your retirement. Finally, after years of demanding work, you have arrived at your retirement morning. Does it seem only a moment ago you left your twenties behind? You were young and energetic. As the first morning dawns, you contemplate the passage of time.

With a hint of annoyance, you wake at your usual time. Yet, the morning seems strange. While the world goes to work, you start your day at home. A feeling of guilt arises as you think of work. You are expecting the boss to call to question your absence. But all is good in the world. You no longer wear the badge of employee.

No more of...
- Having to stay inside when the day is sunny.
- No coworker invading your personal space.
- Endless (and pointless) company politics.
- Being paid less than your clueless manager.
- Overcrowded commuting in the rain.
- Pointless deadlines.
- Having meetings, just for the sake of meetings.
- Drafting reports that nobody reads.
- Uncooperative and depressing co-workers.
- Being refused selected holiday dates.
- Company workload prohibiting holiday.
- Others taking credit for your good work.
- Lack of car parking spaces.
- Late or cancelled train.
- Red tape, just to buy a pencil.
- Lack of thanks for your conscientious work.

We are all creatures of habit. Your daily tempo has been ticking for many years. You set the alarm, commuted, and then returned home. Your way of measuring the day has come to an end. Today is going to be different. Today marks the beginning of your journey to the third age.

Never doubt the decision to retire. If the day begins with a lack of direction, forge small routines. Take a walk on Monday, go shopping on Tuesday, etc. As new ideas pop up, keep a notebook and pen handy to jot down your ideas. Ideas are forever ephemeral; capture them before they vanish.

HOW MONEY CHANGES

From today, how you behave towards money will change. You are going to transition from working and saving to resting and spending. Resting and spending are the two main reasons you saved for retirement.

However, this change will unnerve some. They come to see routine bills as a threat to their savings. The act of keeping money in the bank then becomes a false purpose. To them, holding wealth is important for security and social standing. The habit of hoarding money is an unbreakable habit. Having this balance reduce to pay a humble bill is not something they wish to see.

And yet, money in the bank has no bearing on our physical or mental health. It is the human heartbeat that determines life. Not money. A bigger number in the bank does not embolden a heart.

If possible, embrace good health when you wake up in the morning. View money as a means to create memories and experiences while you can. In this modern age, we are still young at sixty. You have a few more decades to enjoy the third age. While your visits to the doctor are increasing, and your collection of daily pills is growing, celebrate your time-rich retirement.

Remember, you are retired, not expired. There is a later chapter to help you with money and budgeting.

WELCOME TO THE HONEYMOON

No weddings required. Before retirement, you dream of doing nothing all day. You see yourself on the beach, under blue skies, cocktail in hand. And it will be bliss.
After working life, the comfy chair is calling. So, you sit and watch TV box sets. There is a glass of wine nearby.

4 - The challenges

You delight in the relaxation, the decision to retire was perfect. Life after work will become one long relaxing holiday. Retirement was a positive move.

You are in what psychologists call the honeymoon period. The first phase of retirement where the novelty of doing nothing pleases. You can greet each morning with leisure. The day is all yours. Your resting heart rate is down. Take a seat and see the world in motion. Take comfort as you watch others go to work. Watching is one of life's pleasures. After years of having your nose to the grindstone, you are finally free to do nothing. You can sit and rest without care.

Doing nothing or watching TV are only a small part of retirement, however. Doing nothing may serve you well during the honeymoon period, but not in the long term. Clouds will loom on the horizon if this is your retirement dream.

The weekends and public holidays are no longer bookends of the working week. All days have equal meaning and the same amount of free time. The distinction between the working week and the weekend is less defined. A bank holiday, once celebrated as an extra work-free day, has lost its appeal. Sometimes you might even forget what day it is.

As the honeymoon period comes to a close, we realise retirement is for life. It is not the long-term dream holiday we hoped for when working. Doing nothing constructive all day is not the utopia. Boredom is creeping in. The honeymoon period is stalling.

Time to make changes to your day. Time to start a routine that aligns with your new purpose. In the next few sections, we cover building a structure and fresh routines.

Ways to spend time outside the house. To develop new social circles and find new friends. Only you have the ability to initiate the change.

FRESH ROUTINE AND STRUCTURE

As the honeymoon period fades, developing a daily structure will become part of your retirement success.

Until retirement, work provided much of the daily structure. The alarm entered the day at six. You commuted, worked, commuted, ate, and then bed at ten.

Not a hard routine by any means. Even the daily commute helped mentally separate home life from the workplace. But this familiar routine and structure will disappear after working life.

If you chose a phased approach to retirement, the working schedule will melt away with relative ease. Unlike the cliff-edge approach which abruptly halts your daily routine and structure.

Finding a new routine and structure is one of your post-working-life challenges. Yet, to achieve a successful retirement, one must find a balance between being engaged with hobbies and enjoying moments of relaxation. In time, you will master where harmony lives. Meanwhile, the key is to build new routines and structures for your week.

This mantra is worth repeating:

"We must retire from something to something,
and not from something to nothing."

And yet, where do you start?

A blank page
Creating a new routine will take time. Build new structure in small steps. Leave space in the week to explore new interests. Avoid over-committing to voluntary roles that sap away too much free time.

Create a new rhythm for the week. Establish set days for regular activities. These set days are your anchor days. The time in between the anchor days is for free roaming. Time for new things or relaxation.

Take this as an example:
- Monday: explore a local landmark (fixed).
- Tuesday: free.
- Wednesday: art class (fixed).
- Thursday: free.
- Friday: meet up with a social group (fixed).

Here, Monday, Wednesday, and Friday are your anchor days. You have created a structure upon which you can hang other hobbies and activities. Are there any hobbies you could revive? An activity you could coach? Any skills for a voluntary role? Within the structure, you can introduce small routines. Walking to the newsagent to buy a paper. Speaking to neighbours. Even making a to-do list.

Goal setting
Connect your goals with your values. For example, pursuing a degree in diesel technology does not align with a belief in electric cars. Motivation is the foundation of any goal. You will motivate yourself to the challenge and change will happen.

However, along the way, there will be obstacles causing you to rethink the goal. Even to force change. The solution to overcome obstacles is to be flexible. You should not view change as bad. Having to change tack may cause frustrations and derail your ambitions. Think beyond the obstacle.

Suggested goals for retirement life:
- Pursuing a passion to a professional level, such as art, music, or sport.
- Keeping fit and healthy, both mentally and physically.
- Giving back to the community.
- Spending more quality time with loved ones.
- Long-haul travel.
- Leaving a legacy.

Making Change
Question - how many psychotherapists does it take to change a light bulb?

Answer - one, but the light bulb must be willing to change.

If you are resisting change, ask what is being protected by not changing. It is natural to fear the unknown, or to lose control of the familiar. We favour the status quo, and our resistance is there just to protect our comfort zone.

Change can happen if we build small routines into our week, such as leaving the home to meet new people. If reading is your passion, join a book club. The weekly gathering will become part of your weekly routine.
Contact the local U3A (University of the Third Age). A group of like-minded people who come together for a broad range of topics. Is there a local school offering adult classes? Aim to make one day each week purposeful and at a pace that is comfortable.

Voluntary work

Working as a volunteer will give you a purpose and build social circles. But choose a role for the right reason. Volunteering solely for the need to leave the house and socialise may cause frustrations.

- If volunteering career skills, ask how you will feel about working for free? Some retirees come to regret doing the same work with the same frustrations.
- Do you need training? Especially if you are in close contact with vulnerable people and children.
- Will you need personal liability insurance?
- What is the weekly commitment?
- What flexibility is there to follow personal hobbies and activities?
- If working with foreign nationals, do you need to learn a language?
- Could you start on low hours as a tester?
- Would you be working alone or with a team?

Hobbies

A hobby or activity is more than just a way to pass the time. They help to maintain our physical and mental wellbeing, too. For our life after work, they will provide a balanced and satisfying lifestyle.

IMPORTANCE OF COMMUNITY

One challenge in retirement is cultivating a diverse social life. Until retirement, we have grown accustomed to our daily ready-made social group. When we leave behind our working life, a social vacuum may form.

Peter, a director of a medium-sized company, was about to retire. After nearly four decades in charge, he was ready to unwind. Asked what he would miss about his career, his reply was "not much". However, he continued, "I will miss the people at work and those clients I connected with." This director believed retirement would give him more time to spend with friends. But, as he soon discovered, those friends were still working.

A partial solution is to find a reason to leave the home. Staying at home waiting to be discovered rarely helps. Especially when hobbies are solo activities.

WHY WE NEED A SOCIAL GROUP

To be human is to be sociable. Retirement isolation puts mental and physical wellbeing at risk. Being within a social group is therefore important to long-term health. Without it, you may become bored and aimless.

In gentle ways, we can call upon our social groups for support. They comfort us, empathise, and understand when we face misfortunes. Including times when we are sad and lonely. We enjoy the sense of belonging and being connected.

The number of friends you need will depend on your character. An introvert will prefer a few close friends. The extrovert will hunger for a wider social network. There is no optimal number. Dunbar's number says the Ideal count is between one and five close friends. What is important, however, is that we avoid comparing our social life with others'.

Finding friends

Finding friends can be hard. Retirement will bring a shift away from the structured work environment. A place where we meet new people as part of our daily routine. Without working life, we are less likely to have spontaneous social events. Our leisure time has become open-ended with reduced opportunities to meet new people.

As we age, there is a risk of our social space becoming less active. The number of old friends is waning. Some we lose touch with and some move away. Social media helps to a degree, but to find new friends in retirement, we need to push ourselves.

We can meet like-minded people who follow similar hobbies. But these people will still be unknown faces. How best can we prepare ourselves?
- Be open to all conversations.
- Smile - this will encourage others to approach you.
- Actively listen. A stranger will warm to empathy for what they say.
- Stay true to yourself instead of wearing a false mask that will eventually fall apart.
- Be someone who others enjoy being with. A constant complainer will soon find people melting away.

Leave the home, join societies and social groups. Attend events and aim for casual conversation. Be patient - it takes time to become part of a new social group. To make friends, we need to trust and make an emotional investment.

THE ART OF CONVERSATION
Starting a conversation with a stranger is never easy. Feeling nervous is natural. But talk we must. Keeping a conversation going can test the best of us.

The art of a good conversation starts before you even speak. It starts with body language. Think about how you are orientated towards the person. What is your body language saying? Have an open posture and keep a comfortable distance. Are you making good eye contact or scanning the room? Scanning the room sends a powerful message of inattention.

Be ready to listen. Resist the urge to interrupt to put your own point over. Because by doing this, we stop listening and focus on when to jump in. Instead, when they stop talking, mention something they have said. This tells them they have been heard. Knowing they have been heard helps to build a connection between you.

Avoid asking closed questions that can be answered with a simple yes or no. For example:
Question: "Is Paris the capital of France?"
Response: "Yes."
This conversation has come to a halt.

In a similar way, if we ask:
Question: "How are you?"
Response: "I'm fine, thank you."

While we accept this as social politeness, this question has become a modern way of saying hello. It has joined the ranks of closed questions.

Any open question will encourage a response that will kick-start a conversation.

Question: "How are you finding the weather today?"
Response: "Disappointed, I wanted to be in the garden this afternoon

Open questions start with:
- How...
- When...
- Who...
- Tell me about...
- What do you think about...
-

Although you could start some questions with "why," use it with care. Some consider "why" a critical question starter, such as "why did you go there?" Asking what they like is a good conversation starter. And we all like to be validated, even if you disagree with their views. If you disagree, keep your emotions in check and ask whether their view is widely shared.

A balance of participation makes for a friendly conversation. To help you focus, silently repeat their words. Do not let your thoughts stray to the next question. If you are thinking of your next response, your body language may shift to suggest disengagement. Besides, you may miss the importance of what is being said.

It will take several conversations for a stranger to become a friend. Building friendship takes time. Be ready for the unwilling to talk. They may have had a tough day or be shy, or just not be the conversational type. Do not take this rejection personally. Eye contact can be problematic for some. As a partial solution, look at the bridge of their nose instead.

LOSING FRIENDS

Losing friends can be hard and emotional. We will miss friends who pass away, but they remain in our memories. How they had enriched our lives. We can also unintentionally lose friends when we move home, or our resolve to stay in touch lapses. We drift apart. To defend against this, have a routine to call, text, or email. Show friends you still value their company.

For some people, working life may have been too demanding. As they strove to build a career, or perhaps for the pursuit of money, they pushed friendships into the background. Yesterday's good friends have now become acquaintances and, today, rarely seen.

Changing values can also push friends away. As our view of the world shifts, we face conflicts and disagreements. Resolving these new rifts asks us to have an open conversation and be respectful of their perspective.

CONFRONTING SOLITUDE

If we distinguish between solitude and loneliness, few of us will choose to be lonely. Despite being liked, loneliness lingers in a crowded room.

After working life, your social landscape will change. Not only have you retired from work, but your workplace banter has retired too. You promise to stay in touch but, over time, work friends will become acquaintances. Ultimately, work friends will fade away and become part of your past life.

Living longer can also be a cause of loneliness. As life expectancy grows, social circles shrink in later life if we're not careful. Friends have moved away; some have passed away. Some we have lost touch with. Our once vibrant circle of friends has been shrinking for years. Plus, we have our own physical limitations. As the ways of communication change, these technical advances can also be a barrier.

And thus, loneliness is a real sense of disconnection. A condition where we lack friendship and social networks. We feel isolated, leading to poor physical and mental health.

As we live more years in retirement, the number of lonely retirees is growing. Recent data tells us almost 1.4 million UK retirees feel lonely during the day. And if these feelings become chronic, there is a risk of mental health issues. Depression is a common symptom of loneliness. Our lifespan is also influenced. Research tells us the risk to our health is similar to that of smoking or being overweight.

Challenging loneliness
Loneliness does not define who we are. However, we should embolden ourselves and look to change.

The foundations of change are:
- To discover yourself. Reflect on your passions, interests, and core values.
- Not to stay at home waiting to be discovered. The world will pass you by unless you have some social visibility.
- Using daily routines to combat loneliness.
- Overcoming the fear of meeting strangers.
- Boosting confidence by liking yourself.

Liking yourself
Liking yourself is one of the best tools you can use to stave off loneliness. Should you not, your body language will give the game away. Without self-awareness, you can expose your inner feelings. Your eyes, hands, and facial expressions speak volumes. Facing someone with crossed arms is a classic "keep away" message. If you dislike yourselves, how can you expect others to like you?

You will find many books on this subject, including those by Brian Tracy. With a little effort and self-belief, you can greatly improve your self-confidence. Be ready to meet strangers.

Brian Tracy suggests the daily mantra:
"I like myself."
"I like myself."
"I like myself."
If you like yourself, you will be happier when alone and when in company.

ALWAYS STAY ENGAGED

Does new technology make you feel cold and old? Even overwhelmed or frustrated? A simple switch is replaced by a menu. Plug in a new TV and it wants to know your contact details and date of birth! Irritation is universal, but change is unavoidable.

We yearn for the old ways. And yet, two hundred years ago, as steam power entered the workplace, workers feared losing their jobs. They revolted. There was much unrest. Privacy was an issue as the telephone arrived. Workers fought against the Industrial Revolution.

The office underwent a transformation a few decades ago. During the 1980s, the personal computer had arrived. The younger worker was eager for the new technology. A chance to learn spreadsheets, MS-DOS, and the wonderful Edlin.

However, before these computers arrived, there was disquiet among the elders. They had no connection to these things. They were declaring objections and threatening to leave if made to use them.

The computers arrived. The elders left. From the fear of change, they had opted out. Despite their resistance, the computer has revolutionised our world.

Remain in
To remain connected with change means you can have a modern retirement. Today, our smartphone is the dominant device. Without it, connection to friends and family is harder. You can buy devices that monitor physical activity, sleep patterns, and overall health.

Therefore, try not to be intimidated by change. Elect to learn rather than opt out. Treat every change as a fresh learning curve. Remember, all learning is a lifelong endeavour. Learning helps to keep the mind active and healthy as you age. Integrate new technology into daily life.

New technology is not just for the younger generation. By opting in, you can stay connected to their world. Technology will help bridge the generation gap. You can share their adventures. By following change, you keep pace with evolving times and make a contribution to the generations that follow.

THE IMPERATIVE FOR ACTIVITY

Finding inspiration
Finding a new hobby can be hard. But, by staying alert to all the surrounding activity, you make it easier to find a new venture. You may notice ideas are everywhere.

Take, for example, going for an evening stroll to the local pub. There you find a team of Morris dancers. Dancing may not appeal, but you can see it is highly social. Ideas may come from newspapers, magazines or a chance conversation with a friend. The key is to be open to new ideas that may become new passions.

As an exercise, grab a pen and paper and write your best traits. Exclude any related to work. For example, do not list hard-working, conscientious or good timekeeping. Also, exclude the size of your bank account. Consider passions, what brings joy. How do you socially connect, and what is your sense of humour? What makes you happy?

Later, there's a chapter to inspire ideas you might like to explore. If you try a potential new hobby and don't find it enjoyable, that's okay. You don't have to stick with it. Try something else instead; it is essential to be open-minded.

Approaches
Everyone has a unique way of learning. Yet we know that learning something new improves everyone's mental health. Whichever way we choose. Some opt to immerse themselves completely until they achieve expert status. Some people give up easily when faced with frustration.

At the heart of our learning is the brain. An organ with the ability to retain information biologically. As we learn, the brain forms fresh biological neuron pathways. If we surrender at the first frustration and give up, our resilience to non-learning challenges will diminish. If we persevere with our learning, we are more likely to take insightful risk. Taking small risks will serve you well in later life.

Open mind
With an open mind, you have a powerful way to enjoy a happy retirement. Open minds embrace new challenges. With effort and perseverance, knowledge and cognition improve with learning. How we organise our thoughts will improve. Plus, when we face uncertainty, stress levels will be lower. Just like our heart and muscles, the brain's ability improves with use.

Our cognitive health has the potential to last longer if we become a lifetime learner. There is evidence that lifelong learning defends against mental health issues.

Closed mind
With a closed mind, we run the risk of mental stagnation in retirement. Learning new activities holds no value for the closed mind. The closed mind rejects learning. Effort to learn something new in retirement seems pointless. Closed minds hinder learning and brain health.

- Be self-critical.
- Expect negative comments.
- See new things in a negative light.
- Give up after the first mistake.

Remember, we all have a starting point when taking up a new hobby. In every learning group, some members will peacock their advanced knowledge. Others less so. Knowing that we all begin somewhere is key to opening closed minds.

Trying something new is daunting for retirees. People say, "you can't teach an old dog a new trick." They have a false belief that age leads to a static or declining intelligence. The truth is, the learning organ is very good at creating fresh neuron pathways. But only during learning and engagement.

Activities
In a recent study, mature retirees were asked two questions:
- How satisfied were they in retirement?
- How many weekly activities did they enjoy?

The study found up to five activities corresponded with a good level of happiness. Those with one or less showed symptoms of depression. Six or more activities led to a modest increase in happiness. However, ten activities did not make them twice as happy as five.

THE ACTIVITY ARC
The activity arc is similar to the standard deviation curve. A bell-shaped line that rises, plateaus and then descends. The higher the line, the more interest we have in the activity. Across the arc, we find a series of points through which a new activity will flow. First becoming a passion and then parked. A typical activity arc could be:

- The eager anticipation of starting something new.
- The learning curve.
- Progress and improvement.
- A high point of enjoyment, to find a sense of flow.
- The enjoyment plateau.

Having reached the plateau, our new activity will either:
- Become a lasting hobby.
- Lose its power to entertain. We park it to find something new.

Remember, too, at the start of your retirement, you are likely to have good physical and mental health. Over the next twenty years, however, it will decline. You should use good health when you have it.

As a corruption of the popular saying, "use it before you lose it."

CHAPTER 5

ENDLESS PURSUITS

Retirement offers a wonderful chance to explore new things. With our time-rich days, we can enrich our third age. This section lists some of the popular ideas to help you get started.

SPENDING TIME WITH WATER

The Earth's surface is 70 per cent water; the human body is 60 per cent. We relax with the sound of lapping water.

Swimming. Said to be the best exercise. Easy on our joints and helps to improve heart fitness. Ideal for anyone aged forty and over.

Boating. Buying a boat is easy. Berthing and care can be costly. Being on the sea obliges us to:
- Gain an operator's licence for the radio.
- Understand the weather, and when to stay ashore.

- Understand what is under the hull (before we run aground).
- Learn navigation.

Kayaking. To relax, exercise, and find peace in the open water. Kayak designs can be rigid or inflatable. They are all easy to use and lightweight. For faster waters, some models have foot pedals to aid steering. But these versions cost more. Kayaking is an ideal beginner's sport. If you can hold a paddle, you are ready to go.

Water skiing. Ski training centres will supply the equipment, including life jackets. You will need a firm grip, a great body core, and sturdy back muscles. Be prepared for a full-body workout as you glide through the water.

Snorkelling. Being able to swim is not essential; snorkelling is the art of floating. If you make sure the mask fits, breathing should be relaxed. Explore marine life under the waves.

Scuba-diving. Here you can descend deeper for longer. Scuba is the acronym for self-contained underwater breathing apparatus. A risky sport that requires us to be in good health, able to swim, and trained.

Other water ideas:
- Fishing.
- Keeping fit with aqua aerobics.
- A month on a canal boat.
- Kite surfing.
- Exploring the tidal pools.
- Cage diving.
- Paddle boarding.
- Exploring a shipwreck.

ART AND CRAFTS

Art brings together line, shape, form, space, colour, shade, and texture. These are the fundamentals of art. We mix these fundamentals to form our style. Find your niche and explore your corner of the art world. Enjoy the journey. The key is not to craft art just to please others.

Watercolour. The mixing of colour pigments with water. For the beginner, they say this medium is harder to master than others. There is little time for changing colours or composition as the paint will dry quickly. However, the novice painter can achieve excellent results in a short time. Best used with paper having a weight of over 300gsm (grams/square metre).

Oil and acrylic. Unlike watercolour, oil and acrylic take longer to dry. Even when the top layer is dry, lower layers can still be wet. A longer drying time is good news. You have longer to change your work. Canvas is the normal medium, although it can be anything.

Pastels. Similar to sticks of chalk found in schools, pastel sticks are colour pigments held together with a binder. The painting technique is to draw and rub the pastel stick over textured paper. A rougher surface will help with the colour transfer.

Pencil. Whether black or coloured, pencils have various degrees of hardness. A hard pencil will draw a thin line, a soft pencil a thicker, darker line. The range starts at the hardest, 9H (H for hard) to the softest, 9B (B for blackest). The stack of pencils are the tools used for drawing and shading.

Drawing. We often think we cannot draw. Our attempts will offer a vague resemblance to the subject. However, think back to your early school days. Writing was once an epic task but now, as an adult, writing has become effortless. Drawing uses the same dexterity, but differently. If you write, you can learn to draw. Once you have the tricks and techniques, drawing can be easy. The process begins with taking simple subjects and constructing the drawing using smaller shapes.

Pottery. Clay is inexpensive and available at most art stores. However, once you have crafted your creation, you need a kiln. Making pots requires a potter's wheel, too. In the early stages, a kiln and potter's wheel are an investment. However, a nearby art studio may help, or hold classes.

Kit modelling. Do you have fond memories of making models? Today, popular kits remain the same. Cars, ships, and aircraft. Kit manufacturers, such as Airfix and Revell, grade their models. The higher the number, the greater the difficulty. If you have lost some hand dexterity over the years, lower-scale models (1/72, for example) are small and hard to assemble. In recent years, wooden kit models have become popular, too. Kits made by U-gears or Rokr comprise laser-cut plywood ready for fitting without glue or nails.

Knitting. Knitting is back with knit and natter groups. As you knit, you can chat with your fellow knitters. The popular material is wool, but you can knit with hemp, mohair, or jute. There is a learning curve to use the needles correctly. Once started (known as casting on), you can master the basic knitting stitch in no time. Casting on can be a challenge.

Crochet. A needle working technique that uses a single hook to interlock loops of wool. We can find the origins of the name in the French language: croc, meaning to hook. Said to be easier than knitting, and mistakes are quick to correct. With tighter denser stitching, you can produce three-dimensional objects.

Finger knitting. Try your hand at finger knitting. Pun intended there. With dexterity and jumbo-sized yarn, you can craft chunky-knit blankets, scarves, and cat beds.

Whittling. Working with wood is one of humanity's oldest art forms. Thought to originate from early hunting and the need to whittle spears and arrows. For the beginner, softwoods are best. Balsa and pine are easier to cut and contour as desired. Woods with multi-directional grain are harder, as are knots. These small twirls are tricky to navigate and can easily break the work.

Candle making. An easier challenge. The key elements are soy wax nodules, a wick, and fragrance oil. The oil and melted wax are blended and poured into a shaped heatproof container. Before pouring, support the wick to allow the wax to solidify around it. There are candle-making kits with the basic ingredients. Some kits offer a challenge to invent a fragrance.

Origami. The art of paper folding using a single sheet of paper. You create designs and shapes through folds and creases. An art form that requires patience, skill, and creativity.

Card making. Making cards for all occasions. Stamped with your artistic charm.

Calligraphy. Writing to give a sense of grandness to the message. An art form often used with card creation. The art is to create artistic words using a series of thick and thin lines together with curves and swirls.

Creative writing. Words create an image in the reader's mind. You can convey nuances and textures with linguistic skill. Like painting, it has a learning curve to enjoy.

Tie dye. After a decline, this 1960s art is making a comeback. Tie a piece of light-coloured fabric with string and then dip it into a coloured dye. When the fabric is dry and the string removed, a circular pattern emerges.

Blacksmithing. According to the UK's 1850 census, twenty per cent of the working population recorded their occupation as blacksmith. Such was the need for shoeing horses. Spring forward 170 years, only 600 are still with us. To be a smithy, you need upper body strength and tolerance to high heat. An old art form not for the fainthearted.

More art and craft ideas:
- Lace work
- Embroidery
- Felt making
- Quilting
- Tapestry
- Weaving
- Woodcarving
- Wood-turning
- Cabinet making
- Making your own finger paints
- Painted market basket
- Patterned clay trays
- Banner-making
- Friendship bracelets
- Mosaic
- Build a dog kennel
- Soap making

LEARNING FOR FUN

Retirement life encourages us to move in the slow lane. But a leisurely life affects our cognitive thinking. Aim to go beyond essential learning. Experiencing new things and learning encourages the creation of fresh brain cells.

With age, your brain may work differently, but engaging the mind is still important. To become a lifetime learner, you have many options. Colleges and universities run free courses for those over a certain age, either in the classroom or online. Here are some places to explore:

- Stanford online.
- Edx.
- The Open University (OpenLearn).
- The Royal Institution.
- Coursera.
- FutureLearn.

TED (Technology Entertainment and Design).
If you spot a new activity, and it piques your interest, engage with a TED talk. Some universities have free public lectures.

Ancestry. No matter whether your family is big or small, taking a journey through one's own heritage can be both thrilling and revealing. Start by having a chat with the immediate family. Spend an afternoon with a box of old photographs. Put names to strangers. Popular culture tells us that half the UK population has a family line back to a king or queen. Could you be one of them?

FOOD AND DRINK

Cooking. Discover new foods by spending more time in the kitchen. From Malaysian curries to Japanese tempura. From French snails to Middle Eastern spices. Or why not try the unusual, such as black pudding?

Brewing. The cost of equipment is modest. While you can find brewing kits in the best stores, the cheaper kits can pose a taste challenge. Think instant coffee vs. espresso. Try a work experience day at your favourite brewery or visit Germany's Oktoberfest - a festival devoted to beer, polka bands, and oversized tankards.

MUSIC

Instruments. When you learn to play, your memory and problem-solving skills improve, too. Better yet, the brain releases dopamine. Your happy hormone.

Singing. If you have a sense of pitch, join a choir, a band, or become part of the folk scene.

Song writing. Express prose to music. Find the rhythm, add a catchy melody, and build a song around a musical landscape.

TRAVEL

Travel for new experiences. Engage with diverse cultures. In short, we travel to relax, explore, and to learn.

Cruising. This type of travel offers a different port every day. To avoid children, choose adult-only sailings.

Camper van. Dr W Stables first devised the camper van in 1855. A Scottish medic with the urge to travel in the company of home comforts. Two horses pulled his van, named "The Wander", but road conditions often found it stuck in ditches. Such was the quality of the roads at the time. Today, with a camper van, hotels are no longer necessary.

Circumnavigate the globe. You must observe the three conventions. One, travel in one direction. Two, cross all lines of longitude. Three, start and end at the same point. In short, you can travel east or west but not north or south across the poles. Some airlines will sell round-the-world tickets with fixed stops. Or for a leisurely time, cruise liners cater for the adventure, too.

Waterways. Hire a canal boat to explore the slower side of life. Working the locks can be a labour of love. Therefore, having over two people is ideal. Navigating the Caen Hill flight is a challenge - a series of twenty-nine locks on the Kennet and Avon canal that stretches for two miles and can take six hours to complete.

OUTDOORS

In the garden. We can thank the Romans for the English garden. They stylised their spaces with sections of grass, bounded by gravel paths and short hedges. They set aside an area to grow herbs and vegetables. Depending on the size of your garden, here are some ideas to explore:

- Create a themed area (a rose garden).
- Create a seating area.
- Try your hand at topiary.
- Raise some chickens (beware of the foxes).
- Encourage birds to visit with a bird-table.
- Grow hops to make beer (or apples for cider).
- Buy a shed with windows and create an art studio.

Wild camping. Get a real taste of freedom with no amenities. Pitch a tent when the urge takes hold, but you must ask the landowner first. When leaving, there should be no trace of your stay. Have ways to contact people in emergencies.

5 – Endless pursuits

Dogs. Dogs are loyal and good company. Each day, they encourage us to go outside. However, there are responsibilities with owning a dog. Including feeding, training, and maintaining their health. Remember, we have family and friends. A dog will only have you.

Steam train. Sixty years ago, every boy's dream was to be a steam engine driver. Today, that dream can become true with a one-day footplate experience. Shovel coal into a raging fire, wave the green flag, or toot the whistle. Physical effort is required, and your time onboard can be hot, dusty, and arduous. You'll be well chuffed!

Bird watching. Some say bird watching is one of life's greatest gifts, giving us a connection with nature. But this world often remains unexplored until retirement. At a slower pace, we see them differently. As a casual hobby, name the species and watch the dynamics between large and small. And how some guard their food. Begin with a bird table. Better still, make a bird table.

Stargazing. Even with just the naked eye, you can see the moon, constellations, and galaxies. Start with a pair of binoculars to bring them closer. A telescope is ideal. For the best view, keep away from urban lights. No sky is darker than at Tenerife's Roque de los Muchachos Observatory. Artificial light pollution here is under two per cent.

Tour guide. Explore the local area and understand its history, nooks and crannies. The events that formed the towns, country roads, and the people. Both famous and infamous. And with this knowledge, you could be ready to become a tour guide. Well, not quite. You must be an excellent communicator, too. A narrator with presence. Tell a story with energy and performance. A tour guide's role is beyond pointing and telling facts.

Boot sale. In retirement, you may come to see your lifelong collection of stuff as overbearing. Too many things rarely used, cupboards full to frustration. You need the space. Selling stuff at a car boot sale is a popular choice. It is an idea introduced in the 1970s, named after coaching days and the box on which a coachman sat which stored his boots. The car, and the open boot, is a feature. However, sellers now bring display tables and illumination.

GO SOCIAL
You will enjoy any social activity more if the group shares your values. Here are a few ideas to help you take pleasure when leaving the house:

- Volunteer to help at community events.
- Become involved in fund-raising.
- Reconnect with old friends over coffee.
- Start a retirement club for like-minded retirees.
- Try out your acting skills with amateur dramatics.
- Become a film extra.
- Learn to be a magician to entertain parties.
- Wear a period costume and walk around a tourist hot spot (with permission) as performing art.
- If you have an itch to dance, join or start a social dance club. Waltz the night away, shake yourself to samba, or ring the bells with Morris dancing.
- Challenge your thinking by joining a chess club.
- Invite neighbours over on Sunday afternoon.
- Volunteer help at your local hospital.
- Sell your own craft at shows and village fairs.
- Try metal detecting for treasures.
- Join a film club.
- Teaching English as a second language.
- Improve your public speaking.
- Visit a court, listen to interesting cases.
- Thirty minutes in the park observing the world.

GENTLE SPORT

Lawn bowls. Played on a level rectangular lawn known as a green. Two teams hold four wooden bowls. They position a smaller ball, called a jack, at the opposite end to start the game. The goal is to roll their wooden bowls closer to the Jack than the other team. Those bowls nearest the jack score the points. Although gentle, the game takes years to reach league status.

Croquet. Often called lawn croquet. A long-handled mallet is used to knock a ball through a series of hoops. The size of the lawn will dictate the size of the play area. However, the maximum play area is twenty-five by thirty-five metres. The winner passes the ball through all the hoops and hits the stake at the end first.

Fly a kite. While kite flying can be competitive, most of us will reminisce about younger days, beach holidays, and blue skies. With a bit of wind, you can still fly the most basic of constructions. Or design your own and be competitive.

Golf. According to a survey, golf is the most boring sport to watch. Above cricket, bridge, and snooker. And yet, for the retiree, playing golf combines gentle exercise with a social environment. Some say we invented golf for retirement, helping to reduce tension and stress. Others suggest the game is hard to master.

Fishing. Some people fish for sport (returning their catch to the waters) and some fish for food. For some, the main attraction is simply relaxing in nature, not catching fish. While we associate fishing with a rod and line, there are also netting or spear fishing to experiment with.

MEDIUM SPORT

Cycling. As an exercise, cycling is ideal for the older body. You use all the major muscle groups.

Clay pigeon shooting. The clay pigeon is a small circular target made from calcium carbonate and pitch. Launched using a powerful spring, the clay pigeon soars through the air, imitating the flight of a bird. The aim: to hit the clay pigeon with lead shot fired from a doubled-barrelled shotgun. The shotgun uses cartridges that, when fired, project hundreds of small lead balls spreading out as a shaped cloud. Naturally, there are firm safety rules in place for all concerned.

Archery. To shoot an arrow, you need good upper body strength. Firing the first random arrow is easy, but achieving precision takes years of practice.

Windsurfing. The origins of windsurfing are uncertain. Standing on a sailboard, you use wind and a sail to move across the water. A large board aids floating and stability. A small sail makes surfing easier to control and start in light winds. Learning the art is more important than physical strength. Just remember, falling off is part of the learning.

White water rafting. Riding a raft down a fast-flowing river can be an extreme sport. Challenges range from grade 1 (easy) to grade 6 (danger to life). It is rare for people to try grade 6. A life jacket, helmet, and a wetsuit are essential.

Ballooning. When drifting, the world is silent. The only sounds you hear from below are barking dogs.

HARDCORE SPORT

While we have fond memories of being physically robust, the energy and muscle mass we had forty years ago might now be, well, lacking.

ATV. A motorised buggy for uneven and muddy terrain. Whether for work or fun, reckless hill climbing or driving at speed can make an ATV unstable and liable to tip over.

Paragliding. Paragliding is the freedom to soar between the clouds. Launching from a hilltop with flat ground ahead, sturdy lines suspend you under a lightweight fabric wing. Without power, you seek uplifting thermals to take in the sights and sounds below. But before any first solo flight, you will need professional training.

Skydiving. If you seek a rush of adrenaline, you will find it by skydiving. But, along with that adrenaline comes a modicum of risk. It will come as no surprise that you will need professional training beforehand. A jump from 5,000 metres (three miles) will deliver one minute of free fall. Too much risk? Try indoor skydiving for a close simulation.

Cave diving. Diving carries the risk of becoming lost, uncertain of the path to safety or even which way is up. The rewards can be great. Squeeze through narrow tunnels to find a vast underground chamber decorated with stalactites and stalagmites.

RANDOM IDEAS
- Start a new charity aligning purpose with values.
- Study meteorology.
- Learn to fly a small plane.
- Experience a sea-plane landing.
- Visit a train museum.
- Practise mindful eating (take twice as long to eat).

A guide to successful retirement

- Invent a cartoon character.
- Visit a museum daily for a month.
- Play bingo.
- Try skipping as an exercise.
- Lie on the beach and listen to the waves.
- Learn about renewable energies.
- Have your fortune told.
- Complete a 5,000 piece jigsaw.
- Write a children's story.
- Visit a zoo for a day.
- Research your local cemetery.
- Write your own epitaph for your tombstone.
- Sit in the park for thirty minutes.
- Volunteer to teach the disadvantaged.
- Learn to play the piano.
- Have a go at amateur dramatics.
- Write a computer programme.
- Research your family tree.
- Restore an old car.
- Watch a yacht race.
- What was the news on your birthday?
- Learn to run backwards.
- Ride a horse.
- Go to a boot sale and sell your unwanted items.
- Take a scenic bus ride.
- Start a bed-and-breakfast.
- Teach an old dog a new trick.
- Become an expert on Shakespeare.
- Create a website about your town.
- Make your own wine.
- Start a business that gives value to the community rather than for profit.
- Learn to read and understand a profit and loss account and balance sheet of a business.
- Look at the moon through a telescope.
- Renovate a boat.
- Make a documentary for your YouTube channel.

- Sit in the public gallery of your local court.
- Learn public speaking.
- Teach English as a second language.
- Skip stones on the lake.
- Read at least one classic book (e.g. Moby Dick).
- Go on a round-the-world cruise.
- Try painting a self-portrait.
- Revisit somewhere from your past.
- Enter an art competition.
- Volunteer to work in a care home (one day, it might be your Hotel California).
- Visit at least one country whose name starts with each letter of the alphabet, in alphabetical order.
- Put something unusual in your will for your relatives to complete.

SUPPLEMENTING FUNDS

- Start a small business.
- Hold a boot sale (yard sale).
- Sign up for Airbnb.
- Be a secret shopper.
- Sell your arts and crafts.
- Become an eBay trader.
- Self-publish a book to sell on Amazon.
- Sell produce grown from your own garden.
- Become an expert on the foreign exchange or stock markets (only with money you can afford to lose).

CHAPTER 6

DYNAMICS OF A RETIRING BODY

QUICK READ

Without your body, where are you going to live?

This is an intriguing, if not a provocative, question. As we ready ourselves for the journey of retirement, we should ponder on those factors that affect our quality of life. Understanding why we age is the first part of our journey. If we are prepared for our natural ageing, we can embrace retirement with adaptability.

However, we should have the focus of being informed about our body. No need to stress or dwell on certain aspects of your lifestyle. The best option is to try your best. Do not allow your retirement to be overshadowed by anxieties surrounding health. Most times, the media will sensationalise the latest fads and diets to make money.

And yet, being active has the potential to reward us with the health we wish for. Exercise and the right diet are just as important as avoiding excessive toxins.

Taking a morning walk each day is recommended. In doing so, we can boost our mood and reset the circadian rhythm; our body's natural clock. We also trigger the production of serotonin and endorphins, enhancing mood and energy levels.

Our lower body strength will improve, too. With age, falls are no longer seen as comical. Beyond the age of sixty, a fall leads to a risk of broken hips and arms. A fall can even be fatal. Lower body strength and balance exercise will go some way to helping you avoid falling.

The quality of sleep is important for mental health. Equal to the enjoyment of mind games and being a lifelong learner. However, nearly half of us become mentally active at bedtime. We struggle to fall asleep and stay that way. It is normal to wake up a few times during the night. Especially when we reach the end of our natural sleep cycle.

(End of quick read)

PROJECTIONS OF A LIFESPAN

Retirement will bring you moments of adventure. And yet, ageing will bring change to your physical health. But how much we age will, for the most part, rest on our genetics, lifestyle, and the attention we give to keeping good health. Physical health decline is not universally similar. We can also age ourselves just by thinking old.

There is good news. Healthy retirees should prepare for twenty more years of life. More so than sixty years ago, when life expectancy was nearer seventy. And yet, we sometimes perceive ourselves as being old, even at sixty. The brevity of the passing years has placed us into the age once occupied by the grey-haired. Surely, we must be old? The reality is, anyone aged sixty today is still considered young. We still have curiosity, energy and good mental health. Our life is far from over.

WE ARE WHAT WE THINK

It is the nature of the human psyche to define our age by social influences. The media can shape our concept of ageing. Known as stereotype embodiment, our life span can be changed by what we think. How we physically think of ourselves will alter our life expectancy.

As an example, we can mentally amplify our aches and pains. We convince ourselves to spend less time on exercise, saying our bones are too old. We can think ourselves into an early grave.

You happen upon a photograph of your grandma in the 1930's. She has white hair, lived-in skin, and cannot walk without her stick. In the photograph she is sixty-five. Today, you are also sixty-five. Although your physical health differs from your grandma's, the power of stereotype embodiment can be persuasive. If you link your sixty-fifth birthday to her frail image, you may see yourself as older.

When you say "I'm retired" for the first time, you may feel apprehension. After leaving work and wearing the retirement badge, you question whether your usefulness to society is over. As you hear of those younger than you passing away, you question your own life remaining. These thoughts are common but can affect the success of retirement. Being positive and happy is key.

Reshape your subconscious to be young:
- Cultivating a positive outlook.
- Staying active and curious.
- Eating well.
- Maintaining good social networks.
- Having fun and laughing.
- Embracing change.
- Dressing to impress and being confident.
- Nurturing good sleep.

How you perceive yourself is a powerful tool. For the best retirement, remain youthful in mind. And remove those negative perceptions of age.

If we speak to older retirees, they say the first ten years are the best. Ten years ago, their health and fitness were on par with working life. But they did little for learning and exploring. With hindsight, embracing curiosity and energy for a fuller retirement should have been the priority.

OUR BIOLOGICAL AGE

Our biological age is a measure of the health of our internal organs. A nominal age when measured against a common expectation. For example, when we are sixty-five we might expect the biological age of our liver to be consistent with that age. But a sixty-five-year-old lifelong heavy drinker may have a liver with a biological age of eighty.

WHO age groups
The World Health Organisation has tried to put a range to our biological ages. So far, they suggest:
- Underage: - 0 to 17 years old
- Youth: - 18 to 65 years old
- Middle: - 66 to 79 years old
- Elderly: - 80 to 99 years old
- Long-lived: - 100+ years.

This is not the number of birthdays, but our biological age. The World Economic Forum claims we are considered old fifteen years before our life expectancy. Given today this is eighty-two, it would seem we are old at sixty-seven. Being speculative, but is this why the new state retirement age is also sixty-seven?

Research by Milevsky in 2019 tells us:
- A fifty-five year-old Swedish man has a biological age of forty-eight.
- A fifty-five year-old Russian man has a biological age of sixty-seven.

If we lead a healthy life, we can retire on our sixty-fifth birthday with much younger organs. More so than our ancestors of the same age. Life expectancy is growing, and we will enjoy more years in retirement.

How do we know our biological age?
Certain companies specialise in this field. Muhdo Health is one company that offers this service. In 2019, they had a wider public audience when featured on the BBC's technical programme, Click. The programme considered knowing our biological age had a place in helping us

improve our health.

To improve organ age, we should care for our physical and mental health. Stop smoking, reduce alcohol, exercise more, eat the right foods, etcetera, etcetera. Good health is not always under our control, but we have the means to avoid doing the wrong thing.

BODY vs. AGE

There is a balance between self-care and enjoying life in the fast lane. As much as we like to drink, smoke, and sunbathe, an unplanned doctor's visit can bring moments of realisation. Poor health, with no medical fixes, can ruin our retirement.

Body for Life author Bill Phillips tells us to self-care throughout life. To keep active in retirement, we must eat a balanced diet and take regular exercise. This way, we can support our body as we age.

"If you want your body to support you through retirement, then support your body. You have nowhere else to live."
Bill Phillips.

To stay young for as long as possible, we need to reduce our alcohol consumption, stop smoking, and protect our skin from UV light. There is growing evidence to support a good night's sleep, a morning walk, and maintaining the ideal weight are equally important.

DEMYSTIFYING LIFESPAN

We need to age, if only to accommodate our life experiences. Our holidays, finding love, the birth of our children. Ageing is something to be celebrated, not the ruination of life.

That said, ageing is a complex process. We age because our cells, which make up our organs, degrade and die. On average, we each have 37.2 trillion cells. And every day, sixty billion of these cells will stop working. While that may sound alarming, most of these are red blood cells. These have a natural lifespan of 30 days. New blood cells are produced by our bone marrow as each cell dies.

Cells

Imagine a cell is like a balloon. Inside the balloon you find various chemical packages that give the cell energy. You also see a nucleus inside which sits a strand of DNA. It is the chemical sequencing of the DNA that tells your cell how to function.

Thus, the DNA strand in a liver cell will have a different chemical arrangement from a heart muscle cell. When a liver cell stops working, there is a biological process to replace the expired cell.

Stem cells stand ready to replace those cells which have died. But stem cells are blank. They cannot function until they have copied the DNA that lies within the expired cell. However, the number of times a strand of DNA can be copied is limited. Each copy results in a shorter strand. And eventually, it becomes too short. Meaning the DNA strand will break and unwind. Soon, the cell and DNA will be flushed away as they reach the end. No further copies are possible. Over our eighty-two-year journey, the accumulation of lost cells is why we age.

Researchers have tried to extend life by introducing compounds to make our DNA strands longer. One compound, thought to grant eternal life, was added to human cells in a petri dish. But cell division became rampant. Uncontrolled. Should we ingest the compound, we would expose ourselves to a high risk of cancer.

Damaged cells

Every day, the body will replace cells when they become damaged. If we introduce toxins, the rate of cellular damage will increase. The two most common toxins widely available are alcohol and nicotine. Therefore, if we drink or smoke, the rate of cellular damage will increase. Therefore, each time :

- The cell will become damaged.
- A blank stem cell is released to replace it.
- The DNA is copied from the damaged cell.
- The DNA strand becomes shorter.
- The number of times this particular cell can be replaced (with a functioning DNA) is reduced.

If we increase the frequency of cell replacement, our biological age will advance beyond our chronological age.

Water is essential for cellular life. It provides our cells with hydrogen and oxygen, without which the cell has no energy and dies. Too much alcohol dehydrates the liver cell, leading to inflammation and fibrosis. If we consume heavy amounts of alcohol, our liver cells can self-repair (up to a point), but it will eventually fail.

Nicotine places our lung cells under oxidative stress. Proteins within the cell will alter and then fail. Thus, a smoker can have a higher chance of lung cancer.

Sunbathing also plays its part. We need sunlight to produce vitamin D, but too much exposure will harm the skin's cells. For our protection, the body responds by releasing melanin. A pigment that gives our skin the darker colour. If our exposure is too high, the result is sunburn. UV radiation will reach the lower layers and increase the risk of skin cancer.

SLOWING DOWN

The cell renewal process, despite its flaw leading to cell death, extends our lifespan. Longer than most mammals. And yet, we yearn for more life. How can we slow down the ageing process?

The following is not medical advice, but from literature in wide circulation.

- Follow a diet that includes antioxidants.
- Take regular exercise to reduce oxidative stress and improve blood flow.
- Manage stress with relaxation techniques.
- Protect your skin from the sun.
- Avoid or reduce toxins, such as alcohol or smoking.
- Have the right amount of sleep.
- Maintain a healthy weight.
- Avoid high-processed foods and excessive sugar.

Stopping our cells from dying is not yet possible. Eternal youth still evades us. However, following the common advice above may give us a longer retirement. One day, we may find the secret to extend the human life span.

Imagine not retiring until you are 150 years old!

POWER NAPS AT HOME

We tire for many reasons. However, in early retirement, the change away from our work routine can also play a role.

Routine

Retirement brings ample free time that changes the structure of our days. We aim to ease routines and adopt a more relaxed approach. However, without any routine, our days can become rudderless. With no set routine, our physical and mental activity is at risk of decline. Being rudderless and lethargic can lead to tiredness.

Brain
If you are bored and aimless, you will feel tired. Likewise, the lack of mental stimulation adds to your fatigue. The solution is to use each half of the mind in turn. There are two minds that exist within the brain. A left hemisphere and a right.

The left hemisphere is linked with our logical thinking. It helps us to solve problems and process language. It also controls the right side of the body. The right hemisphere is the creative side. That part of the brain that leads us to be artistic, to have intuition, or to be aware of what is around us. It also controls the left side of the body.

While both minds bring their respective strengths to the table, if you are overusing one side and feeling tired, stop and use the other.

Sleep
Tiredness will arise from a disruption to our sleep pattern. Ideally, you should aim for a steady sleep schedule. Even on the weekend. The key to good sleep is consistency. A uniform sleep pattern will regulate your internal clock. Eating late does not help, and drinking alcohol before going to bed will disturb the sleep cycles. We'll look more closely at these later in the chapter.

Exercise
Lack of exercise in retirement gradually reduces stamina. While relaxing is our reward, too much slouching is not ideal. If we exercise for twenty minutes a day, feelings of tiredness will reduce. Plus, we may improve our life expectancy.

Food
Making poor food choices will crash your energy levels. While food can become a comfort, eating fast food late at night is not ideal. When eating, pay attention to what your body is telling you.

Water
Dehydration will make you feel tired. How much you drink each day will depend upon your exercise levels, the climate, and age. A common suggestion is to consume two litres daily.

Medications
It is known that our biological efficiencies change as we grow older. Therefore, review your medications with the doctor. These may be out of balance with your needs.

VITALITY OF IMMUNITY
It is also certain that our immune system will weaken with age. As the thymus shrinks, the ability to fight infection declines. The body's immune function will weaken.

Our immune system relies on the production of white T and B blood cells. Manufactured within the bone marrow, they surge into the bloodstream and lymphatic system.

While they are described as white, these cells are colourless and extremely small. And their numbers are vast. We produce one hundred billion white blood cells every day, with an average concentration of 7,500 cells per micro-litre of blood.

The role of the white blood cells is to remove known viruses. To help with this, we can train our immune system with vaccinations. Called adaptive immunity, this is the marvel of biological life. It adapts and grows to fight a wide range of dangers while avoiding healthy cells. And thus, while these white cells are unceasing in their work, we can enjoy retirement life.

However, after the age of sixty, our ability to defend ourselves declines. As white blood cell production falls, we become prone to infections. We see changes too. Wounds are slower to heal and our response to infection is slower.

Support
To keep your immune system fighting fit:
- Have the right amount of exercise.
- Follow good nutrition guidelines.
- Stop smoking (smoking has the greatest negative impact).
- Keep within safe levels of alcohol consumption.
- Have the right amount of good sleep.
- Accept all vaccines offered.

Cold shower
There is a widespread belief that a short, cold shower each day will help boost the immune system. A burst of cold water will trigger our natural fight-or-flight response, causing the immune system to surge. White blood cells flood the body. The method is to have your normal shower with the final 30 seconds on a cold-water setting. However, there is a warning. Avoid doing this if you have an overactive immune system - generating extra white blood cells is not recommended in this situation.

Perfect slumber
Sleep has an important daily role. It makes our biological clock tick. And yet, nearly half of us struggle with this nightly routine. The enemy of sleep is anxiety. Not only do we become mentally active when reaching the pillow, but we become anxious over our quantity of sleep.

Let us dispel two sleep myths
Meeting an eight-hour sleep target is unnecessary. While falling short of eight hours can cause anxiety, eight hours is an average, not an instruction. The healthy range is between six and ten hours. Therefore, the right amount of sleep is whatever suits you. As we enter retirement, as we age, our quantity of sleep changes.

The second myth is that we should have our dose of sleep in a single session. This is not correct. From historical records of the pre-industrial age, we see patterns of segmented sleep. Individuals enjoyed two periods of sleep, with quiet activity in between. Today, we become anxious if we wake during our eight hours. Waking is normal. Thomas Wehr (known for his work on circadian rhythms and sleep) theorised that we wake at the end of each sleep cycle to check for danger.

NEW TIME
How we change our relationship with the morning alarm must be one of the greatest joys of retirement. There is now silence where once we rose for the early hour. But, for all our Anglo-Saxon mutterings, the morning alarm gave some routine harmony to our day. Now you're retired, your daily routine will change, which will vary your sleep pattern. Thus, before changing your routine, you should know your chronotype. This is the body's natural preference for when to be wakeful.

There are three chronotypes:
- The lark: Most productive before noon. Ten per cent of the population are larks and will prepare for bed before eight pm.
- The dove: Sixty-five per cent of the population are doves. Doves are most productive between ten am and two in the afternoon. They wake at

seven am and prepare for bed before eleven pm.
- Night owl: Feel at their best in the evening. Twenty-five per cent of the population are night owls and will often still be active after midnight.

Your chronotype will depend on a mixture of genetics, age, and when you first see natural light. Becoming a night owl in retirement if your the body prefers the morning may cause upset. At least at first.

Your role in sleep is simple. You fall into it. Once in bed, sleep will start within twenty minutes. For the older retiree, hormonal changes, muscle pain, and medical conditions make this stage harder.

The quality of your sleep will influence the quality of your retirement days. Equally, the time you spend asleep will support, or tarnish, your wakeful time.
- Under five hours will impair mental clarity.
- Six to eight hours is considered best.
- Over ten hours, we become sluggish the next day.

At the extreme end, if you were to deprive yourself of sleep for two days, your mental function would decline. There would be mood swings, cognitive decline, and, finally, hallucinations.

RHYTHM
Having the right amount of sleep is one consideration. The rhythm of our sleep is another. It is called the circadian rhythm.

The circadian rhythm has been with us since the birth of humanity. A natural biological clock that aligns our daily activities with the environment. As the sun rose, we knew when to go hunting and expect food. As the sun set, we knew when to sleep. Today, your biological clock will still respond to the hours of light and dark. Thus, by keeping with your circadian rhythm, you will stabilise mood and hormone levels.

The rhythm of the night is a blend of our circadian rhythm and our sleeping pattern. If we change our sleep routine, we push against the circadian rhythm. As a result, we wake feeling jet-lagged. Our feeling of being fresh and ready for the day has gone. Our biological clock is out of step with the twenty-four-hour day. Medical opinion says good sleep is essential for good retirement. But how do we define good sleep?

Good quality sleep requires passing through three unique stages. Together, we call these three stages a cycle. And each stage within the cycle has an important part to play. The quality of each cycle is important, not the time we spend asleep.

We can disturb these stages by eating late, consuming alcohol just before bedtime, or restricting our sleeping hours. It is also known for sleeping pills to affect our sleep stages by suppressing REM sleep. While they help us with insomnia, sleeping pills can fragment the natural sleep cycle. Either of these things will lead us to have poor sleep. We will feel under par the following day.

In retirement, establish a regular hour for bedtime. And one for the morning, too. Resist the long lay-in every morning and find natural light to reset the circadian clock.

Stages (REM: rapid eye movement)
0: Transitional
1: Non-REM - light
2: Non-REM - deep
3: REM sleep

Transitional
This first stage is temporary. It is the transition from wakefulness to light sleep. Your heart rate is slowing. Breathing is shallow. Your muscles are relaxing. Eyelids close, eye movements pause. We have little awareness of this phase. Should someone wake you, you would deny being asleep. But your eyes are closed.

Non-REM - light
At this stage, the brain enters a time of high electrical activity. You are easily woken at this stage. Your senses will respond to any noise or nearby movement. Any dreaming is short-lived and has no real story narrative. The electrical activity between the neurons is helping you to retain learning. Light non-rem sleep is said to be the most important stage.

Non- REM - deep
Now, your brain activity is flowing in waves. Delta waves. You are fully relaxed. Your heart rate is slow, but the brain stays active. You are now at a crucial stage. The brain is regenerating. Consolidating memories and releasing hormones to regulate growth. Without this stage, your thinking becomes cloudy. Next day, you would be forgetful, irritable, and gloomy.

REM sleep
Following the two non-rem stages, you enter the final stage, REM sleep. As brain activity increases, you enter the dreaming stage. Under your eyelids, the eyes are moving. Thankfully, you cannot move your limbs to act out your dreams. REM sleep helps you with daytime creativity and finding solutions.

Nightly routine
Dreaming is complex and dynamic. Each night, your sleep will cycle through these stages. During a seven-hour sleep, you may journey through four or five cycles, each lasting ninety minutes, and you may briefly wake at the end of each.

Each night, the average sixty-year-old would spend:
- 25% awake.
- 50% in light sleep.
- 10% in deep sleep.
- 15% dreaming.

Sleeping and cleaning
Recently, it was found the gap between our brain cells grew during deep sleep. As fluid floods between the cells, it washes away waste protein and dead cells into the bloodstream. Removing brain waste will help us feel less anxious the next day and lowers the risk of Alzheimer's.

While you have little feeling of being asleep, how you feel the next day reveals your sleep quality. Long-term poor sleep will present some symptoms, including:
- Loss of short-term memory.
- Loss of or lower insulin control (type 2 diabetes).
- Decline of the immune system.

None of the above is to suggest that you should avoid late nights or early mornings completely. No harm will occur in the short term. But long-term and continuous sleep deprivation will degrade the quality of retirement life.

NAPPING
There is no greater retirement pleasure than an afternoon nap. Having a nap in the afternoon is normal. Napping is common and part of daily life in certain countries. In

Spain, the siesta is a tradition dating back centuries. The reasons you nap can vary, but it is known that the circadian rhythm makes us sleepy in the early afternoon. A successful nap has a few elements:

- Avoid napping for longer than thirty minutes. More than this will cause sleep inertia when waking. A period of feeling sluggish and not fully revitalised.
- Aim to nap between one and four in the afternoon. During this time, your body temperature naturally drops, and there are chemical changes causing you to be lethargic. Which have a mild soporific effect. Avoid napping too late in the day, which can disrupt nighttime sleep.

To help avoid a nap:

- The morning meal should be a balance of protein, fats, and complex carbohydrates. A meal of simple carbohydrates give you a quick burst of energy.
- For lunch, avoid foods that are high in sugar and refined carbohydrates.
- Get some simple exercise in the afternoon.
- Balance how you use the brain during the day. Problem solving engages the left side of the brain, while painting uses the right.

SLEEP APNOEA

Sleep apnoea is the relaxation of the upper airway. The soft tissue here comes together and causes sufferers to pause breathing during sleep. The airway is obstructed. In severe cases, this happens up to forty times an hour. According to the National Sleep Foundation, 20 per cent of the population has sleep apnoea. And yet, 85 per cent of these people are not aware of having the condition.

As breathing stops, the brain wakes. Not fully, just enough to restore breathing. But now, the sleep cycle has been interrupted. The next day, sufferers spend their time feeling tired and unfocused. Sleep apnoea is medically serious. Suffocation is rare, but if it is not treated, health will suffer. In serious cases, someone can perish in their sleep. And 15 per cent of car accidents each year result from drivers falling asleep at the wheel.

Symptoms before being officially diagnosed can include:
- Loud snoring.
- Paused or stopped breathing while asleep.
- Being woken by choking or gasping for air.
- A tendency to fall asleep throughout the day.

Your partner may also comment that you appear to stop breathing.

It is common for alcohol and obesity to trigger the condition. One solution is to use a CPAP machine at bedtime.

A CPAP (continuous positive airway pressure) machine is a medical device that provides a constant stream of air. This air has a slight pressure to keep the airways open. It requires wearing a mask, making sleep less comfy. But the benefit arrives the next day. You feel more alert and less fatigued. Those who are treated say they feel twenty years younger.

NATURAL LIGHT

Take a walk in the morning sun
To boost our day-to-day mood, a regular morning walk is the recommended choice of exercise. This can be done at an intense or gentle pace, allowing us to reset our circadian rhythm. We know this rhythm as our natural body clock and this time of each day has an importance for our physical and mental health.

6 - Dynamics of a retiring body

You may be surprised to hear that our natural body clock does not run to the standard twenty-four-hour day. It is fifteen minutes longer. And thus, over the course of eight days, our natural clock will silently drift by two hours. The consequences? During the day, our tendency to nap increases. At nighttime we have insomnia.

To reset our body clock, we need to expose ourselves to natural light. Natural light is a mixture of seven colours that combine to produce daylight. You can see these colours when sunshine and rain come together to form rainbows. The blue light (which is part of natural light) is the wavelength that helps us reset the body clock.

As darkness arrives, blue light falls. As a result, melatonin production increases, preparing your mind and body for sleep. In the morning, the reverse is true. With more blue light, melatonin reduces. We become alert and ready for the day.

But in this modern age, we now expose ourselves to blue light long after the sun has set, from our screens and artificial lighting, which suppresses the production of melatonin. Our modern way of living is disrupting our circadian rhythm and leading to sleep disturbances. Melatonin is the rhythm of the day. More at night, less in the morning.

The morning walk will help you reset the circadian rhythm. As well as melatonin, natural light will also trigger the production of two further hormones:
- Serotonin, which calms us and makes us feel happy. This is why we find serotonin in antidepressants.
- Endorphins to help with problem-solving and creation of memory.

A one-hour brisk walk within two hours of waking is ideal. You can even walk before sunrise. Twilight on the horizon means there will be blue light surrounding you. We reduce melatonin and increase serotonin and endorphin levels. If you make this a regular exercise, you will feel differently about your day. Feel happier and more energetic. This holds true in summer with longer daylight hours, but not in winter when lethargy sets in.

Research by the Ulster University found the best walking speed is between 100 and 130 paces per minute. A brisk pace that causes us to be breathless, but still allows for conversation.

They also found aiming for the target of 10,000 steps a day encouraged exercise. There are health benefits to walking. We can manage our weight as well as reducing the risk of heart disease. However, not all steps are equal. Slow steps (when shopping, for example) will not give the same exercise value as brisk walking.

ALWAYS STAY UPRIGHT

In our younger days, falling over may have been seen as comical. We take the knock, stand up, and continue with the day. Falls have varying concerns as one grows older. From the age of sixty, we are more at risk of injury. Our bones are less dense, making them liable to break or fracture. If we break a bone, medical intervention is needed, and it takes longer to heal. During the recovery, our muscle mass decreases, and we lose our mobility. A fall in later life is no longer comical.

For the new retiree, physical strength is good. There is a low chance of falling. However, The World Health Organisation says that each year, 684,000 of us will die by unintentional falling. Broken hips, knocks to the head, or internal bleeding are the common injuries. Rarely do we have any advance warning. If we fall, we suffer the injuries. To guard against a fall, stay active with a routine of exercise, know your physical limitations, and improve balance.

BALANCE

Our balance comes from a blend of senses. Using sight, muscle tension, and organs within the inner ear, the brain orientates the body to stay upright. But, as we age, the speed at which our brain can merge these signals slows. Likewise, our reaction time to stop a fall will lag, too. From the age of thirty-five, we sometimes feel dizzy. Our ability to remain upright degrades. Therefore, one ingredient to reduce the risk of falling is to maintain the speed of the brain. The faster the brain can blend the senses, the faster you can stop a fall. Balance training will help with this.

Balance training

For two minutes each day, stand on one leg. This simple solution could add years to active retirement life. Integrate balance training with other routines. Waiting for the kettle to boil or brushing your teeth. Electric toothbrushes will often have built in timers that can help with the duration.

With something to grab nearby, raise one foot off the floor and bend the lower part of the leg back. Looking ahead (not down), aim to stay that way for twenty seconds. Return the leg to the floor and repeat with the other leg. Balancing for over twenty seconds is a sign of a healthy brain.

With age, our brain relies more on our eyes for balance. Therefore, as an added challenge, stand on one leg with the eyes closed. If you stay that way for over ten seconds, you are doing well.

If standing on one leg is proving difficult (even with the eyes open), try the tandem balance. Imagine standing on a tightrope. Place the heel of one foot in front, touching the toes of the other. Stay in that position and then swap legs. We should aim to make balance training a routine before falling becomes a problem.

Tai chi

With graceful movements, the art of Tai Chi helps improve bone strength and stability. With slow movements, the head rotates at different times from the body. Making us focus on leg strength, flexibility, and the need to stay upright.

THE HEAVY BURDEN OF WEIGHT

Even if for years we have followed a good diet and eaten the same number of calories each day, we can still gain weight in retirement. This is because the number of calories our body burns is governed by our metabolism. And your metabolism is changing.

After thirty, our metabolism will slow down by 5 per cent every decade. Hence, there is a latent risk of having more body fat in our sixties than in our twenties. And yet, at the start of our retirement, we stay agile for a few more years. Even when carrying these extra pounds. With advancing years, however, the price we pay for this extra weight will take its toll.

Carrying too much weight in retirement will cause health issues. High blood pressure, diabetes, and knee pain. We have the added risk of developing sleep apnoea, too. As we saw earlier, this condition causes poor sleep quality and fatigue the next day.

As we carry more weight, our level of activity falls. We find our joint pain restricts mobility further. We enjoy sitting to watch the world go by instead of walking. And as our physical activity declines, calorific burn falls too. As we lay down increasing amounts of fat, we risk becoming overweight.

That said, the correct weight is not about having a slender body. It means keeping to a weight that is right for your height and body type. And which allows you to live a healthy and active lifestyle.

In retirement, we have more time for self-care. If we build an exercise routine from the early days, we will build muscle mass and increase our bone density. Having a higher bone density will further help protect the hip from breaking should you have a fall. Mortality rates from broken hips are not low.

"Those who think they have no time for bodily exercise will sooner or later have to find time for illness."
Edward Stanley, the 15th Earl of Derby.

Increasing rate
Here are some ways you can increase your metabolic rate:
- Have an exercise routine.
- Eat more protein foods. These require extra energy to digest.
- Get the right amount of good sleep. Having too little can reduce the metabolic rate.
- Stay hydrated to help metabolism to function.
- Avoid stress, which imbalances hormonal levels, which can affect the metabolic rate.

While these suggestions may help, genetics and other factors can also play a role in the metabolic rate, so results will vary.

The World Health Organisation says 1.2 billion people in the world are obese. Of these, 2.8 million will pass each year.

FAG BUTT OF HEALTH
What happens to us when we smoke?

We smoke to seek a hit of nicotine. An addictive chemical that enters the brain, triggering the release of dopamine. Dopamine is a happy hormone and is the reason most smokers smoke. We drink alcohol and lose our fortunes to gambling for the same reason. We crave this oasis of dopamine and relaxation.

While smoking is giving our dopamine reward, nicotine causes the heart rate to increase. Smoking reduces the percentage of oxygen in the blood. The heart wants to deliver the right amount of oxygen for our body. But as nicotine enters the bloodstream, the heart must circulate more blood. It beats harder and comes under stress. If we increase our heart rate this way for extended periods, our risk in life is cardiovascular disease.

When smoking, toxins enter the lungs - for example, carbon monoxide, benzene, and tar. As the lung cells are starved of oxygen, damage is certain. The ability to expel infections reduces. The risk of chronic obstructive pulmonary disease (COPD for short) increases. Currently, there is no cure for COPD.

Longer term effects
The nicotine hit will enslave us. Smokers will continue to smoke, knowing that the habit will harm their lungs, heart, and skin. Carbon monoxide will reduce blood oxygen saturation. A smoker's skin will be dull, inducing wrinkles; they will look older than their years.

A heavy smoker is someone who puffs over twenty cigarettes a day. The evidence reveals a poor mortality rate for heavy smokers. On average, their life expectancy will reduce from eighty-two to sixty-nine. That is a loss of thirteen years. If they retire at sixty-five, a huge chunk of retirement life is at risk. Twenty-three per cent of smokers will not reach their sixty-fifth birthday.

The number of people who smoke has been in decline since 1974. From a high of 46 per cent of the population to 13 per cent in 2022.

According to ASH (Action on Smoking and Health), "It is estimated that the global yearly death toll as a result of tobacco use is currently over 8 million (including exposure to second-hand smoke). It is predicted that by the end of the 21st century, tobacco will have killed one billion people within the last century. ASH goes on to say half of all smokers want to quit the habit.

Giving up
Our physical and mental health does not need nicotine to function. Therefore, to have a long and happy retirement, giving up the dopamine hit will improve our chances. Like all addictions, there will be challenges to overcome and the cravings. While there are many books on the subject, in high regard is Allen Carr's Easy Way to Stop Smoking.

Benefits
In time, our lungs will heal and return to normal. Here is a general timeline for lung recovery after quitting:
- Within eight hours, the carbon monoxide level in our blood drops, and oxygen level increases. We feel less lethargic.
- After forty-eight hours, our sense of taste and smell will improve.
- After seventy-two hours, the bronchial tubes are

relaxing, making it easier to breathe.

- Within the next twelve weeks, our blood circulation improves and lung function increases. There may be less coughing and shortness of breath.
- After one to nine months, the cilia in the cells regain normal function. This can reduce the risk of lung infection and the ability of our lungs to oxygenate blood improves.
- In just one year, the risk of heart disease is reduced by half compared to a smoker.
- Within five years, the risk of stroke drops to that of a non-smoker.
- Within ten years, the risk of lung cancer falls to about half that of a smoker.
- After fifteen years, the risk of heart disease matches that of a non-smoker.

If anybody wants to have a long and thriving time in retirement, giving up nicotine should be top of their list. If you're a smoker, ask yourself - what would the future you be saying today?

CHAPTER 7

MENTAL AGILITY

QUICK READ

Keeping your mind in trim.

Understanding how the mind changes with age gives us a useful edge in retirement. We ask, in this chapter, how does the brain function decline as we age? Is mind happiness the secret ingredient to a longer life?

Happiness comes from living in the present, not dwelling on the past or future. But hidden within all of us is the reticular activating system - a bundle of nerves that influences our thoughts, behaviour, and happiness. If we follow Buddhist wisdom, we may believe we are what we think.

It is natural to compare ourselves with others. But not healthy if we draw negative conclusions. This ambushes our retirement happiness. Especially if we are trapped in a pessimistic conversation with a "poor me" person.

For the best brain health, we should aim to become a lifelong learner. Contrary to widespread belief, the brain's ability to create new cells continues in retirement. This means we can still learn and enjoy new experiences. Exercise and avoiding a harmful diet are important, too.

There are risks with our newfound free time - boredom. The dangers of boredom are real for those unprepared for retirement. Some even abandon retirement. Returning to the workplace solely to keep busy. Others go in the opposite direction; they overwhelm themselves with excessive activity. The fear of doing nothing can hijack a retirement as well. The key is to find a balance between the edges of your comfort zone as you keep the mind and body active.

(End of quick read)

THE FLOW OF HAPPINESS

On a scale of one to ten, how happy do you feel? You may find this question hard to answer, but research tells us there is a close correlation between being happy and living longer. When we are happy, we are encouraged to self-care. When happy, we follow healthy pursuits and take regular exercise.

The Chinese philosopher Lao Tzu tells us:

"If you are depressed, you are living in the past,
If you are anxious, you are living in the future,
If you are at peace, you are living in the present."

We can take Lao's philosophy and relate it to our time in retirement. He is warning us about the difficult moments from our past that may compromise the present. And the risk of losing present happiness that arises from future anxiety. Finding peace with the past and the future is key to a joyful retirement.

PAST

During quieter moments of retirement, we may look back at our past. Times when life was hard or angry. A divorce, legal issues, or financial hardship. Today, we might avoid certain places in case we meet these people again.

These moments are small scars on our emotional landscape. A poison that can flow into retirement, causing disquiet and unhappiness. We remain forever tied to these moments, as if by a thread spun by the Fate sisters. Until we untie the thread, we are trapped by this bonding. For a happier retirement, we must unbind the thread. And we achieve this through the power of forgiveness.

When we forgive, we help ourselves, not the aggressor. When we choose to forgive, we become empowered to untie the thread. We have broken our bond and freed ourselves. As the thread falls away, closure arrives.

Remember: we cannot change the past. When we embrace closure, we allow living in the moment to appear.

PRESENT

Living in the present requires us to slow down the pace of life. Age has given you the time to slow down. Reflect on the essential aspects of life. Retirement brings the lack of rush. By allowing a slower pace of life, we sense a deeper connection to our special third age. This is what retirement is for. Consider a task that we might think we have to endure. A train journey to see Grandma.

In our mind, we board the train with the sole purpose of reaching point B. As we focus on the arrival at Grandma's house, we see the journey as an endurance. We find it boring because we take no interest in our surroundings. And then, the train suffers a delay. It holds us back for twenty minutes. When we arrive at point B, Grandma will hear about our stressful journey.

If, instead, we engage our senses, our awareness of the journey will change. As the train moves along, look out the window, people watch, welcome the sounds. There are announcements, track noises, and other people's conversations.

By slowing down, we increase our awareness of the present moment. The journey may be common, but today this train ride is exclusive. Every clock tick is unique and is consumed from a limited source. This train ride, and our time, will never be repeated. With retirement, we have opportunities to transform our common journey into something enjoyable.

Be intentional in how you spend your time. Think about the things you might say to yourself when reaching the last of your days. What do you regret not doing? Is there a wish to pursue an interest that needs a certain level of younger fitness? Overworking is a common source of regret.

Unhappy

At times, we can find ourselves unhappy in the present moment. Regardless of our location or activity, we find disappointment and boredom. Why does this happen to us? The major cause is because we are passive. We wait for an external source to entertain us, to make us happy. And yet, perfect moments exist every day. Never wait for that perfect moment but make each moment the best that it can be.

Comparisons

It is part of the human condition to compare ourselves to others. We use our subjective benchmarks to see our place in the wider world. We ask, what status do we have? Are we successful? Are we richer?

Comparisons serve a purpose in daily life, yet there are traps to avoid. We focus on what we lack, not what we possess. With the wrong focus, we create a retirement that is unfulfilling, fuelled by a fear of missing out.

The fear of missing out (FOMO) is from our false perceptions of others. We associate happiness with having a bigger house, a newer car, or an attractive partner. Rarely is this true. A stranger's life remains unknown to us.

That lovely couple we met on holiday appeared to have the perfect life. But behind closed doors, their marriage was in torment. We only saw a veneer of contentment that was masking an unhappy marriage.

Someone will always have a bigger house, newer car, or more stunning partner. In contrast, someone else will own an older car, live in a smaller house, and have a partner of questionable character. Comparing ourselves to others is not always a pathway to a happier retirement. A friend who parades a yacht in the south of France should inspire us, not make us unhappy.

Talk

One key to happiness is talking to strangers. Talking without fear will transform your engagement with the world. By increasing your social interactions, you improve the quality of your time with friends and family. You will be calmer and less stressed. Talking to strangers (without fear) is a challenge, but you will feel connected socially. The largest social prison you can create is inside your own mind.

GUARDIAN OF THE MIND

Located near the brain stem is a bundle of nerves that has an influence over our thinking. We are not aware of this, but these nerves have a say over what the brain needs to know. These nerves are called the RAS, the reticular activating system. By sensing our surroundings, they will have influence over our behaviour, arousal, and motivation.

For example, imagine you are at a party full of chatter and music. Across the room, someone speaks your name. Above the noise, they catch your attention. This is your RAS on autopilot, sorting through the party's white noise.

The RAS filters out information that can be safely disregarded. Then someone speaks your name. Sensing its importance, the RAS allows the sound of your name to pass through.

Overall, the RAS is good for our mental health. But there is an unforeseen side effect. Mainly on our level of happiness.

THE RAS EFFECT

To help us navigate the world, we use our thoughts. But where do our thoughts come from?

In our early years, our parents or caregivers influence our view of the world. Some events are positive and engaging, but others were negative and distressing. Adults teach us how to react to both.

Then, as a young adult, we mingle with friends. We gather in groups that are like-minded. While retaining the world view given to us in childhood, we blend those thoughts with the perceptions of our new social groups. Outside these groups, we watch current news, media, and other social influences.

All these things come together to help us understand the wider world. But the RAS has some control over how we respond to news and events. Just like a party, not everything we hear reaches our cognitive thinking.

Take these two scenarios:
- If we perceive the world as a good place, the RAS will support that view. We pay more attention to the good news, and not the bad. We are positive and happy.
- If we believe the world is a bad place, the RAS will suck in bad news. We are not happy.

While all this might seem tenuous psychobabble, there is a key point here. From Buddhist teaching we have the proverb, "You are what you think."

Such is the power of the mind that we can induce a state of happiness (or unhappiness), just from our thinking. Many people do not fully appreciate the mind's power. We are in control of our thoughts. If we think bad things will happen to us, they will. Or, at least, we magnify our misfortunes, dwell on them for far too long, and make ourselves unhappy. Taking the psychobabble a stage further, there are some who believe it is our thoughts that create reality. They say all thoughts have energy and connect to an energy field for the collective consciousness, creating the world. A step too far?

Media
News and media are (broadly) biased towards bad news. And because of this unfair representation, we are compelled to believe our world is forever bad. There are a million good deeds for every piece of bad news. Good deeds performed by good-minded ordinary people that go unseen. The world is good, not bad. To be happy in retirement, avoid becoming sucked into the media's negative world.

Retraining the RAS
Thankfully, we can retrain the RAS:
- Try to focus on the positive things.
- Find and express gratitude.
- Choose to be with positive people, not cynics.
- Pursue those activities you enjoy most; other fun activities will follow.
- Replace the morning grumps with a daily affirmation.

These ideas are not overnight solutions. It will take time for your RAS to direct your thoughts to a positive track. But the more you do, the more your RAS will pull in positive experiences.

Being positive also enhances resilience to a setback. This is why people bounce back from bad news. Their mindset is always positive. They stand up, dust off, and get on with their lives.

You could try this daily affirmation:
Today I am healthy.
Today I am wealthy.
In the warm sun, lapping warm seas.
I'm enjoying the company of good friends
that surround me.

THE ACTIVE MIND

Daunting as it may seem, for most of us, our mental health will slowly degrade with age. One defence is to keep the mind active and thinking.

Our brain is infused with eighty-six billion specialised cells called neurons. Neuronal communication enables the brain to function as a unified organ. We have cognitive thinking. This is the mind.

Neurons

A neuron is a single brain cell. When a neuron is born, it will be receptive to learning for several years. This means it is never too late to learn, even in retirement. The neuron will, however, eventually die, to be replaced by a new cell. Although thousands of new cells are born daily, not all survive.

The cells we have will control our thoughts, mood, and senses. Our brain will deliver our actions. How we perceive the world and enjoy retirement is determined by our thinking mind.

But, after the age of sixty, the rate of cells dying outstrips the birth of fresh neurons. We can still learn but, as the years pass, our brain mass is shrinking. This is why we find it harder to remember passwords or telephone numbers. Or even where we parked the car!

Just as our heart is essential to circulate blood, our thinking brain is the powerhouse of the body. And while the neuron is king, we also need the flow of hormones for the brain and body to function.

THE HORMONES

The brain uses hormones as messengers. They flow away from the brain to the target cell and affect that cell in some way. If the vast number of hormonal messages change, we change too. This change is the real plight of retirement and ageing.

The four main hormones the brain uses for communication are:
- Dopamine.
- Endorphins.
- Serotonin.
- Oxytocin.

Dopamine
The purpose of dopamine is to help with our physical movement. But with ageing, our level of dopamine will fall. We become prone to Parkinson's disease. However, not all of us will suffer from this degenerative illness.

We often know dopamine as the happy hormone. When levels are high, there is a sense of reward and pleasure. Before retirement, we may have received promotion or felt proud of our accomplishments, for example. During these times, our dopamine levels increased, making us happy. After our career, the production of dopamine can be less frequent.

After our working days, there may be moments when we feel aimless. We lack motivation and are bored. During these moments, we can artificially stimulate this happy hormone with common drugs. But there are dangers.

These drugs are nicotine and alcohol, and they increase the dopamine level artificially. They give us a false sense of happiness. Although these two drugs are legal and in wide use, they can pose a danger to health.

Gambling is another way to stimulate dopamine. When we win, we are happy. If we lose, we harm our finances. The addictive nature of these things stems from their ability to create happiness. However, excessive use can harm our retirement health.

Endorphins
The primary function is a natural pain reliever. The flow of endorphins is like dopamine. If we increase our level of endorphin, we receive a sense of pleasure and reward. Increasing our levels is easy if we exercise, such as running 5-km or working out for thirty minutes. Those who raise their levels this way will often refer to it as the "runner's high". They experience a sense of euphoria and gain a positive outlook on life.

If our lifestyle becomes sedentary, our level of endorphins will fall. As a result, we find our mood lower and have cravings for comfort foods.

Having a low level of endorphins is rare. Symptoms include aches and pains and mood swings. We may develop an addiction to euphoric substances, such as heroin or cannabis.

Natural ways to boost our endorphins are:
- Moderate to vigorous intensity exercise.
- Comedy and laughter.
- Our favourite music.
- Consumption of dark chocolate (though there is limited evidence on this).
- Sexual activity.
- Dancing.

Serotonin

We have serotonin to calm our mood. But it also helps with our memory and sleeping pattern. While the gut produces most of our serotonin for a healthy digestion, the brain needs a small portion.

After a working life, if we feel isolated or lonely, we risk a fall in our serotonin levels. Depression or anxiety may follow. We are prone to mood swings that some mollify with alcohol. However, if we seek to calm our mood this way, our emotions will usually intensify. To help, doctors will often prescribe anti-depressants. And there is limited evidence that eating nuts, eggs, and cheese will help too.

Oxytocin

Oxytocin helps us bond with a social group. In the workplace, we call this bonding the team spirit. However, this hormone also helps us have an emotional attachment to our friends and family. We feel good when in a relationship. Thus, with some affection, we also call this the love hormone.

Where oxytocin levels are low, we lack empathy. There is also a risk of autism and depression. Reduced levels of this hormone are rare.

KEYS TO HAPPINESS
We all share the same longing for happiness. And yet, most of us are unsure about what truly makes us happy. Sometimes we see happiness in a fun activity. And yet, we often find ourselves unhappy, despite being surrounded by amazing life experiences. Why is this?

What is happening here?
We can define happiness as being calm and peaceful. It is found in the simplest of things. A blue sky, the sound of rain, or a good cup of coffee. One could argue that happiness is simply the opposite of being unhappy. However, a closer definition would be the alignment of life events with our expectations.

In modern times, the media and advertising suggest that something is lacking in our lives. Happiness is marketed as something we can quickly buy. So, we buy with the expectation of finding happiness, but we fail. Because the stuff of our lives has no inherent quality to make us happy. Including money.

The mistake lies in assuming that happiness hinges on certain conditions and prescribed actions. We believe our happiness has to be gained. So, we take our expensive holidays or drive our new cars to be rewarded (we hope) with happiness. It works for a while, but we soon return to our status quo. Believing we are no longer happy, we try again with the next must-have the media machine puts our way. And so, the cycle continues.

Happiness is the natural state of feeling safe, calm, and peaceful. When our surroundings are safe and secure. When we are warm and well-fed. Happiness comes from appreciating the little things. Like the sound of rain.

The factors that bring happiness can be unpredictable. The sound and freshness of rain can bring us happiness if we are warm and under cover. Especially if a rainbow appears. However, if we are having a picnic on the beach, the same rain will dampen our spirits. The same event with different happiness states. That the same event can lead to contrasting states of happiness or unhappiness tells us there's an additional factor at play. That factor is our expectations.

If the events in our daily life are meeting expectations, then we are happy. If we feel an event is not meeting our expectations, or not going our way, then we become unhappy. When we know what our expectations of events are, happiness in our life will become consistent.

Happiness lies in our thoughts, not the event itself. Hence, we can take our expensive holidays and still be unhappy. When we do not get what we want (or expect), we can become unhappy.

UNHAPPINESS

Unhappiness is a common experience in life. Unhappiness and negative emotions are a form of self-protection in the short term. When the brain is not at its best, it suggests the need for change. With no change, we risk our mental health. The human condition (to promote self-protection) is that we dwell upon our unhappiness. We repeat the event in our thoughts and may even embellish our unhappiness with false scenarios. If we stay in a state of unhappiness for a long time, we suffer.

Until we take positive steps to move out of unhappiness, our brain has the unique ability to replay the event that caused the unhappiness. The brain wants us to be happy again. Returning to a time when daily life met our expectations. Do nothing, and we endure continual rethinking.

The first step is to acknowledge the event that caused the unhappiness. Then remove any embellishments. For example, following an argument with our partner, we may add the embellishment that they no longer love us.

This is not true. Do not let something untrue make you unhappy.

Next, can you do anything to fix the unhappiness? For example, if the train is late and you are going to miss an appointment, fix your unhappy state by calling ahead. Once we take steps to fix the unhappiness, our brain will move away from the emotional negativity to thinking and problem solving.

But sometimes there is no solution. Unhappiness caused by the loss of a loved one has no fix. We hate life for doing this to us, but we can change nothing. It is part of living. Have committed acceptance of the event. Stay engaged in acceptance by taking small steps each day. Until we engage with our unhappiness, it will not go away.

STATES OF HAPPINESS

When we are happy, our bodies respond in ways that promote our overall wellbeing. While happiness alone will not give us a longer life, we can take steps to reduce stress and other ailments. But, as simple (and obvious) as it sounds, wanting to be happy is necessary for our happiness.

Daily life is calm and peaceful. We are in a neutral state of mind, free from unhappiness. It is safe to be in a neutral state. We are at peace with the day and ready to enjoy our activities.

Within the boundaries of our expectations, our hobbies and activities will move us away from this neutral state. They will make us feel good or be something that we value. They bring happiness to our day.

Therefore, within all of us, we can experience:
- Feel-good happiness.
- Value happiness (short-term).
- Value happiness (long-term).

Feel good
We feel good about a moment, chemical hormones within us change. The change rewards us with happiness. For example, enjoying a TV programme or browsing the internet for shopping. But, within a short while, our hormone levels return to normal. We are back in our calm state. Repeating the moment (say, TV watching) may bring satisfaction but, after a while, seeking happiness from the same source can cause frustration. Playing golf is a good example.

Value (short term)
Like our feel-good happiness, short-term value-based happiness comes from pleasure with a short shelf-life. Buying into trends or the latest fashion is a good example. We are happy to peacock our new clothes with friends as it helps us bond with the wider social group.

However, when trends and fashion change, what we have will cease to excite. We return to our neutral state, waiting for the next craze. Older retirees (in the last years of life) dismiss trends and fashion. These have no value. The greatest value now is more time.

Value (long-term)
Long-term value-based happiness is the satisfaction we gain from experiences. Experiences that are in tune with

our life values, or arise from fresh adventures.

Either will provide us with rich memories. We can re-live our experience in thought and in conversation. We can use our experience to enhance our knowledge. This is why travel is high on the retirement bucket list. We plan, we engage, and we retell:
- Before (anticipation and excitement).
- During (living in the moment).
- After (memories, retelling the experience).

From experiences, you can create memories to last many years. They instil a sense of fulfilment that will endure throughout your retirement. More so than watching box set TV or shopping.

It is important for the new retiree to avoid the money trap. In spending on travel and experiences, we fear our wealth will expire before we do. So, we stop spending. To reduce our anxiety, we focus instead on saving. Our readiness to spend has set boundaries.

While these thoughts are concerning, saving too much curbs our longer-term happiness. We should consider both saving and enduring happiness in equal measure.

HUMOUR
We develop a sense of humour from a very young age. With young eyes, we observe the world. Our young mind can understand simple physical humour. We laugh at the simplest of slapstick. Punch and Judy or Tom and Jerry are great examples. We even laugh before talking.

Twenty years later, our humour has matured. We wrap humour within context, culture, and intelligence. We pay to watch comedy and are ready to laugh at a great joke. We make others laugh with our own sense of humour.

Laughter floods the body with endorphins. A powerful feel-good hormone on par with morphine. In retirement, we can enjoy life by observing the natural humour of life. Be ready to tuck away a fun story. A stock of yarns to recount when in company. Having a good laugh will make us feel younger. Our frame of mind, our mood, is positive. When meeting strangers, humour and laughter are universal. They even cross language barriers.

How happy we are in retirement depends on our willingness to be happy. However, research by Dr Sonja Lyubomirsky has found our happiness is a mix of:
- 10% our life circumstances.
- 40% our thoughts, words, and actions.
- 50% our genetic make-up.

Her discovery that half the reason we are happy is down to our genetic makeup may seem surprising. However, a 2011 study found higher life satisfaction with those having the 5-HTTLPR gene variant. In 2016, a further study involving over 300,000 volunteers confirmed her findings.

This gene is not essential for happiness. Those with the gene had higher life satisfaction. The rest of us rely on the remaining fifty per cent: circumstance, thoughts, words, and expectations.

UNHAPPY MINDSETS
Just as we hope to avoid being unhappy, we should deflect our negative thinking, too. Thinking negatively can become habitual to some. They fall into the habit of looking for the negative rather than the positive. Those with a negative mindset may find retirement gloomy. And yet, we naturally think about our flaws and then compare ourselves with others.

Making comparisons
We compare ourselves with those around us to shape our self-image. To understand the reach of our abilities and intelligence. This is how we discover our place within society's norms. We also make comparisons with our former selves. We reflect on yesterday to better ourselves today. Thus, by making comparisons, we encourage self-improvement and strive to be equal with our peers.

However, there is an ambush. We pay more attention to those who have higher status. We regard them as being more intelligent, overflowing with popularity. In short, they are having the life we desire. During moments of reflection, we feel a sense of failure because of these thoughts. We self-ambush ourselves into a dull, unhappy retirement. We are internalising the negative influence.

The reality is there will always be those better off than us. People, lifestyles, and wealth will always differ. Without this, we would lack uniqueness.

To break away from negative thinking, express gratitude. Think about what you have today. A peaceful society, a healthy life, family, and friends. Express gratitude for what you have. Not what you do not. With a shift of perspective, you can restore positivity.

Imperfections
The media often presents a perfect world. The body-perfect to challenge our own body image. A standard against which we contrast and consider what is normal. But the media, in all its forms, presents a false norm. It is relentless with the unattainable. Air-brushed beauty standards, flawless lives, endless perfections. We feel insecure with these messages. We question whether we are imperfect.

True perfection lies in our unique imperfections. Being imperfect makes us perfect. Those around us will give little regard to a wonky nose. In fact, to some, a wonky nose is appealing. We are all unique, not social media clones. Our imperfections make us more human.

Circumstantial
Sometimes, we are unhappy because of where we are.

Imagine this common scenario:
We are in a store ready to pay and leave. But we are instructed to stand in a queue and be delayed. As we wait for our turn to pay, there is a flash of annoyance, but acceptance. Our level of stress may rise. Being asked to wait gives a sense of being pushed aside.
To a small degree, we are experiencing disrespect. But all we can do is wait. So, we wait with the desire to be treated equally. We also expect to be treated fairly in our wait.

The waiting time frame is subjective. Extended waiting will affect our calm resolve. Stress and discomfort bubble up. We become angry. Flustered and irritated, we spoil our day. The solution can be simple.

As we stand in line, choose to live in the moment. Remember, we are retired. We have ample time to pause our day. To be curious about our surroundings. Standing in line is another form of pausing. Listen to sounds or watch people. Time flows constantly, but retirement enables us to savour the present. Do you really need to hurry?

The past
A painful past can follow us into retirement. It survives with a link that creates fear. Fear that it will happen

again. Often, we will bring the past into the present day. We can also live in the past by hoping for change. Or searching for reconciliation. So much so that it becomes a constant habit. A condition that can become anaclitic depression (a type of attachment or separation depression). Current activities provide little enjoyment for those with the condition.

Leaving the past behind is hard. Understanding that we cannot change the past is crucial for a happy retirement. If we live in the past hoping for closure, it may never come. There may be no apology. We should accept the past as part of our history. Use the power of forgiveness. Forgiveness does not mean forgetting. When we forgive, we let go of the past. No more anger, resentment, or bitterness. Until we do, we will not fully appreciate the present day. If we spend our time living in the past, how will we live in retirement?

The future
Our brain can also anticipate future events. We can prepare for the future while enjoying the present. This is good. We can find happiness today and see a new tomorrow. To find a romantic partner or a holiday of a life-time. By thinking ahead, we create a sense of longing and anticipation. Thinking ahead can be a powerful motivator.

However, there is another ambush. Chasing tomorrow's happiness, we forget the present day. The expression "I'll only be happy when x happens" is a good example. Waiting for something to happen shifts our retirement life to the future. We no longer live in the present moment.

What we do mindfully today regulates our thinking for tomorrow.

"Happiness is not something ready-made. It comes from your own actions." Dalai Lama.

UNHAPPY HABITS

Life of boredom
If we find life repetitive, and without true challenge or engagement, our retirement will bore us. Retirement becomes a rut, and it will only get deeper. Only one person can use the ladder to climb out - yourself. Explore new activities, grab those signature opportunities, leave the comfort zone.

Pessimism
Believing bad things will happen is often self-fulfilling. Pessimistic thoughts are hard to overcome, but we must see them as illogical. Our first step is to challenge the facts. Look for the evidence to support our thinking. Without evidence, we expose our negative thoughts as false. If proved false, our pessimism will evaporate.

Staying at home
Staying at home gives us a chance to enjoy our own company. However, staying at home when we become bored with our own company is not ideal. We risk reducing our social interactions to the point of loneliness. Our mental health may suffer. The key to a fulfilling retirement is not to stay at home. Join clubs or travel groups. Sign up for evening classes, workshops, or volunteer. Be ready to leave the house and mingle.

Complaining
We complain to express our annoyance. Sometimes frustration. We may complain in concert with others or go

solo. Complaining serves a purpose with friends and family. A way to seek sympathy or validation. A way to suggest a problem needs attention. Complaining too much, however, will lose us friends.

Missing opportunities
If you hear an opportunity knocking, answer the door. Your comfort zone may go screaming out the door, but opportunities are the lifeblood of retirement. Take a risk and jump. Not all opportunities will excite you, but they will add freshness to your daily routine.

PEOPLE WHO DRAIN US
Those who have a bias towards negative thinking will live in negativity. But there is a strange twist here. They use negativity to attract pity. They use pity to gain attention. Attention that cannot be gained from personality or achievements.

Sounds harsh, but these are the "poor me" people. They will often play the victim's card and are seldom happy. They think the world conspires against them. Their expectations for life are big. When their lifestyle does not meet these expectations, they believe life has a single purpose - to treat them unfairly, to give a life of continuous bad luck.

The poor-me person is addicted to personal drama. They present their hardship to seek emotional support from their social group. And, for a moment, they hold court and bathe in the attention. They will:
- Talk about how hard life is.
- Encourage us to endorse their stories.
- Seek our agreement that the world is a bad place.
- Enjoy their level of misery.

They find fault in most things. Sapping a jovial mood out

of any pleasant conversation, they look for empathy. They become a sympathy drain. Blaming external factors for their problems, they resist finding solutions. They would rather dwell on the bad, rather than seek ways to improve. The longer we spend with a poor-me person, the more their outlook on life can rub off on us.

A typical conversation may start as:
- "I saw the new show last night. It was awful."
- "I went shopping yesterday. It rained all day."

A poor-me person is toxic to a happy retirement. If they complain, change the subject. Set boundaries and be clear about which topics are on the table. And most of all, never agree how awful life is.

We have the power to choose who surrounds us. Negative people will attract negative people. Stay positive and be with positive people.

Gentle negativity
It is human nature to defend ourselves against possible unfavourable outcomes. If we are playing cards, for example, we may say "I'm poor at cards" and then lose the game. Saying in advance that we are poor at cards is self-defence. Not negativity.

ENGAGING THE INTELLECT
In later life, learning becomes a matter of brain preservation. Before retirement, we had a clear incentive to learn. We committed our free time to studying because the benefits were bright and clear to us. For our career, for promotion, and to increase our pay.

On the day of retirement, we are still alert and perceptive. Then, over the coming decades, our brain and mind will slowly deteriorate.

The best defence we have against this decline is to try fresh activities and become a lifelong learner.

THE BRAIN

Learning in later life is possible because the brain continues to generate new cells. However, a single brain cell cannot think by itself. It gains thinking ability by connecting to millions of other cells. And to connect with all these other cells, our hormones play a key role. Without hormones, thinking is impossible. The two important hormones are dopamine and serotonin. Dopamine is the brain's messenger telling us how to move. The other, serotonin, regulates our attention and behaviour.

As we age, our body will produce less of these hormones. When production of dopamine falls, our movement is impaired, making our day-to-day activities difficult. We know this condition as Parkinson's disease, which harms around ten million people worldwide. Our memory and cognition will weaken too.

We may find:
- Our ability to learn is slower.
- Multitasking will become harder.
- We have slower memory recall.
- We forget appointments.
- We have a lower mood (or depression).

Alzheimer's and dementia are not part of ageing, but could affect us in our later years. Dementia affects around fifty-five million people worldwide. With longer life expectancy, it is anticipated this number will increase.

Regardless of what we do, our brain health will undermine the quality of our retirement. However, we can slow the speed of the decline if we:

- Take regular physical exercise.
- Are socially active.
- Ensure we have a healthy diet.
- Getting the right amount of quality sleep.
- Be a lifelong learner.
- Do activities that are intellectually stimulating.

That said, we can speed up the decline by drinking too much alcohol or experiencing lifestyle diabetes, obesity, or poor sleeping patterns.

Until recently, it was thought the number of brain cells became fixed on reaching adulthood. It was thought that the cells died slowly over the decades, never to be replaced. Current thinking (sorry about the pun) is that our brain will produce new cells. With new cells, the brain can form new pathways.

Learning
By learning, we create new connections and pathways in the brain. Hence, we can delay the decline of brain health. In our later years, we may be slower, but we can still learn. Being artistic or learning a new language increases connections across different regions of the brain, for example.

Here are a few simple ideas:
- Use your non-dominant hand to open doors. When actions become automatic (such as opening a door with the dominant hand), fewer pathways are created in the brain.
- Read aloud, rather than using the internal voice.
- Stop rushing and allow time to observe the world. Slowing down allows us to explore new opportunities.

Find games that require concentration and attention, such as those offered by www.lumosity.com.

- Learn to draw, paint, or anything with a visual aspect. It helps the mind understand what the eyes see.
- Learn a new language to fluency.

BRAIN EXERCISES

Brain exercises are great for passing the time of day. And for our mental stimulation. However, once we become familiar with the challenge, we lose the benefit. Meaning, while we enjoy our Sudoku and crosswords, the rate of creating new pathways in the brain reduces. And if new pathways decline, the benefit of brain exercises goes down, too. If we stay within our learning comfort zone, our goal to slow brain ageing falters. Therefore, we need to be a lifelong learner. To try new things for mental stimulation continuously.

Flow

Flow is a positive mental state. We are so captivated by an activity that nearby sights and sounds fade into the background. While in flow, we ponder less on the problems of the day. When we become absorbed, the flow has arrived.

Flow is like meditation. It calms our natural fight-or-flight response. When experiencing flow, dopamine levels increase and stress levels decrease. Our sense of time becomes distorted.

Avoid

Learning is perfect for brain cell growth. With growth, we slow the decline of our mental health. However, don't do any activity just to relieve boredom. It will rarely fully engage us should you have indifferent interest. Likewise, avoid any learning that is too challenging. That leads to frustration. While we can become enthusiastic about learning, we also need to make room for those new ideas that come our way.

Have control of the end reward. For example, if the goal is to write a novel, there may be disappointment ahead if publishers reject it. As they often will. Write a novel but self-publish. Or don't publish at all - write it just for yourself and friends.

A FLAT LIFE
Boredom. To be bored is to retire from the third age.

An abundance of free time can pose challenges for the new retiree. We are healthy and relatively young. But we are still willing to waste our days doing nothing. However, boredom is close by when we do nothing.

Each day begins with the rising sun. How we enjoy that light is for us to steer. Therefore, do we become bored by the lack of guiding authority? Remember, our day was once governed by work.

New retirees who become bored often return to the workplace. A 2017 study discovered that approximately twenty-five per cent of new retirees return to work to combat boredom. But it was not always this way. According to a 2016 study, one hundred years ago boredom was rarely a health issue. With a lower life expectancy, time in retirement was often brief.

Today, life expectancy has grown to give us a new term of life, the third age. Twenty extra years to explore, work-free. But our surplus of time brings the risk of boredom. After one year, some retirees feel isolated. The slower pace is not the long holiday they imagined. Without a purpose after work, their days are boring.

Afterwork
As we saw earlier, at first, every day brings freshness. After years of work, we can finally relax and enjoy ourselves. We call this the honeymoon period. But the honeymoon period will not last. Each day merges into an endless measure. Then, it dawns upon us that:

- The end-of-the-week Friday feeling has gone.
- Public holidays are no longer special days.

Becoming bored will be the ruination of retirement. Unless we plan and foresee the content of our days, we discover there are forty hours of doing nothing. Those expecting retirement to be a never-ending holiday will soon encounter boredom. What should have been the dream, instead becomes tedious. Those unprepared for retirement can find it to be their own worst enemy. Extended periods of monotony and boredom can be a painful experience, if not chronic.

PROCRASTINATION
The art of procrastinating is one reason we cannot lift ourselves out of boredom. We procrastinate by looking for perfection. From the fear of performing badly, we linger and waste our time.

Procrastination will often come from feeling bored, leaving us underwhelmed and never satisfied. Even a hobby that we once enjoyed has lost its stimulus. Frustration sets in, our mind disengages, and we resist the activity. Procrastination is winning. The best of us can be plagued by this state of mind.

When procrastination is winning, we focus on the path of least resistance. Just to be doing something. Watching TV is one such path, but not a solution. Watching TV is the friend of the procrastinator. They say television is my only companion. But a TV friend cannot engage with them. They listen to TV stories, but they cannot debate ideas. There is no emotional feedback or warm touch.

Our boredom frustration will remain:
- If we lack the motivation to do something, we delay action.
- If something lacks value, it stays on the to-do list.

Overcoming procrastination can be hard. But there are ways to break free:
- Divide the task into smaller chunks. With manageable pieces, the project is achievable. We feel less overwhelmed.
- Set goals that are measurable.
- Create an action list that will never run dry.
- Rank all tasks in order of importance.
- Begin with the hardest task on the list. After that, the rest is easy.
- Set a timer and work without interruption.
- Silence telephone, email, and media notifications.
- When a minor task pops up, do it straight away.
- Every task on the to-do list must be unconditional.
- Resist doing something just to kill time.
- Identify the right direction to catch goals and desires. If we are aimless, boredom may soon appear.

Immersion
Sometimes we can over-immerse ourselves. We stay busy for the sake of having something to do. But we soon find being busy can also lead to boredom and frustration.

We fill our day with voluntary work. Take a part-time job. Or walk next door's dog even though we prefer cats. We find none of these things fulfilling or rewarding. Our free time is consumed. A common pitfall for retirees.

What matters most is feeling fulfilled. By being fulfilled, we have energy. Fulfilment gives meaning and purpose to our days. Whether we are sitting on a beach, talking to a friend, or flying away to a holiday destination.

When living in the moment, have a party in the mind. Immerse yourself and enjoy. Unless we have high immersion, little satisfaction will flow from any activity. Nothing will release us from boredom faster than discovering a sense of purpose.

GOING BEYOND THE ZONE
Making our comfort zone larger will enrich our retirement.

It was author Judith Bardwick who first coined the phrase 'the comfort zone'. Originally, the use was to highlight the entitlement mentality found in the workplace. Today, however, we use the phrase to describe a state where we feel safe and secure.

Although it's not a physical space, our comfort zone is a place where we see familiar routines and activities. Our environment is stable and predictable. We are free from stress and anxiety. We are happy to stay in our comfort zone.

And yet, we need to leave our comfort zone for new experiences. We can plan or have unexpected experiences by leaving our comfort zone. But if we don't push the boundaries, we will limit our retirement activities.

There will always be some risk. Stepping out of a comfort

zone means embracing uncertainty. As we push against our boundaries, we may feel uncertain. This is common and natural. Should we push too hard, our fear will turn into panic. And if the panic becomes too strong, we push back. We return to our comfort zone.

PUSHING AGAINST THE GATES

We have seen a new activity and are preparing to leave our comfort zone. But these gates (we call them gates of frustration) block our learning path. We push against each gate. Some gates will only need a gentle nudge, others a kick. These gates should never dissuade us. They are just momentary setbacks on the path towards the larger goal.

Once we have reached our goal, we have created a larger comfort zone. We have infused new skills, increasing our resilience to times of change. We have kicked away boredom. Any setback now becomes an opportunity.

CHAPTER 8

ALCOHOL AND GAMBLING

QUICK READ

What are the dangers if we dance with these two vices?

Our love of alcohol and gambling can lead to addiction at any stage of life. Only in retirement do we face the combination of ample free time and the need to combat boredom. Excessive alcohol will steal our health; gambling will rob our financial security.

As we age, our liver's ability to process alcohol declines. The more we drink, the stronger our liver seems, but this is a false perception. Our brain hormones are adjusting to the effects of alcohol.

After the first drink, we sense a delay in receiving the dopamine reward. Thus, we are self-encouraged to drink more.

While alcohol may give us relief from loneliness and boredom, it poses health risks. Alcohol stimulates hunger, so we gain weight. If the pancreas becomes inflamed, we risk type II diabetes. If we use alcohol for sleep, we disrupt the natural sleep cycle, leaving us tired the next day. Caution is needed for those who make alcohol part of their retirement lifestyle.

Gambling can be entertaining, but it carries the risk of addiction. Especially for bored retirees seeking a new purpose. Beating the odds and winning triggers a rush of adrenaline and dopamine. While it is true that these two hormones help us forget our bored state, we are soon back to square one. As the high fades, we are self-encouraged to seek bigger wins with bigger bets.

(End of quick read)

SHADOWS IN THE WINE GLASS

The liver's ability to remove alcohol from the body will decline with age. The rate of metabolism will slow, meaning you will become drunk sooner. Which may not seem that dreadful, depending on your point of view.

Alcohol can help us escape loneliness and boredom. And yet, when sobriety returns, loneliness and boredom will still be with us. We do also link drinking with certain activities. For example, when on holiday, reading a book, or socialising. We may think life without alcohol will taint these activities. Not so. You can still enjoy these things without alcohol.

When we mix age and alcohol, the main health issues are weight gain, type II diabetes, sleep disturbance, and liver damage. Although the change in tolerance levels will be gradual, keeping below safe levels can bring rewards in later life.

Weight gain

Hunger is stimulated by alcohol, causing us to snack and eat more. Alcohol will also delay the trigger that tells us when to stop eating. Alcohol is calorific and is used as energy. As an easier source of energy, the body will use calories from alcohol first. The excess calories (mostly from the food) will be stored around the body. And with age, as our metabolism slows, so does our storage of fat grow. We gain weight with increasing ease.

Lifestyle diabetes (type II)

Diabetes is a disorder of the pancreas. Without this organ, the body loses control of the blood sugar level. Blood sugar, or glucose, is a critical source of energy for all our cells. If the cells lack energy, they are impaired. So too will our health be in retirement. With sustained alcohol consumption, the pancreas becomes inflamed. Its function degrades and then fails. The pancreas cannot self-repair. If this organ fails, we require insulin to keep the correct blood sugar level.

Sleep

A small drink before bedtime can make us feel warm, relaxed, and ready for a night's rest. However, drinking alcohol before bedtime is not ideal. A drink may help us doze off but, once asleep, alcohol will disturb the natural sleep cycle. Alcohol will impair the quality of our sleep. We feel tired and groggy the next morning. Try a couple of alcohol-free days and see how you feel the next day.

Liver

We associate heavy drinking with liver damage. While the liver is a robust organ and can self-repair, the onslaught of alcohol will eventually take its toll. If we lose over thirty per cent of our liver function, self-repair will pause. What remains of our liver to function may not cope. The liver may fail. As gruesome as this is, there are few warning signs.

YOUR BODY'S RESPONSE

If you are a regular drinker, is your tolerance to alcohol increasing with age? Do you now drink more before feeling tipsy? The reason is not because your liver has grown stronger. Instead, your brain is adapting to alcohol.

Although we often associate drinking with the liver, it is our brain that gives us the reward. The reward of relaxation and the feel-good factor. But this reward results from hormone disruption in the brain. And the brain fights back to restore balance.

Just as our liver works hard to remove alcohol from the blood, our brain works equally hard to restore hormone normality. As the brain delays the reward (which it will), we drink more. Therefore, if alcohol is part of our retirement lifestyle, we should have some caution.

After a working life, we have ample free time to cultivate new drinking routines. At any time, we can choose to relax in the afternoon sunshine with a glass of wine. But as our brain counters the effects of a single glass, we have another. Just to reach the same feel-good factor. In the worst scenario, we may have a glass of wine in the sunshine at 2.30, finishing the bottle by 5.30. It never used to be this way! So, what is happening?

After the first drink
When alcohol enters the bloodstream, our liver responds to remove it. And rightly so. In biological terms, alcohol is a poison. And yet we enjoy the effects.

Alcohol is first absorbed in the stomach. Depending on its contents, roughly twenty per cent of the alcohol will enter the bloodstream from here. The longer alcohol stays in the stomach, the longer it takes to feel the desired effects. Thus, if we drink when eating, the absorption rate will be slower. Since the first drink had little effect, we pour another. We have been fooled into drinking more.

Next, the alcohol will move into the small intestine. From here, the absorption rate will increase, but the alcohol flow will still be directed towards the liver. The liver will soon be overloaded.

The liver's response
Alcohol is now flowing in the bloodstream and making its way into the liver. As the alcohol arrives, the liver will metabolise it. But, because the liver cannot cope with the flood of alcohol, a proportion will flow back into the bloodstream. The presence of alcohol in the bloodstream

causes a shift in the brain's hormonal balance. This is the reward we seek.

While we may enjoy alcohol, its presence in the blood is problematic. Alcohol is toxic to our liver cells. These cells become inflamed and their function impaired. The oxygen level within the red blood cells is also falling, meaning we risk cellular damage to our organs. Especially the heart muscles, which are now working harder.

Not all of us will suffer liver damage. Much will depend upon consumption volume, genetics, and duration. Only the liver can eliminate alcohol. Without this organ removing alcohol, we would fall into a coma, with death not far behind.

The brain's response
The brain is not happy. But we are. As alcohol crosses the blood-brain barrier, the hormonal levels needed for proper brain function are about to be disrupted. And yet, it is this hormone disruption that sustains our relationship with alcohol.

Dopamine
The production of dopamine will increase. This is the happy hormone. As dopamine floods our reward pathways, our confidence grows. We feel less stress. We can gain relief from boredom or anxiety.

GABA
The activity of GABA (a calming amino acid) reduces. As a result, we slur our speech and have less co-ordination.

Glutamate
As the activity of glutamate (a neurotransmitter) reduces, our thinking will slow.

While we crave for these hormonal changes, our brain is going to fight back.

Fighting back
While we can control our drinking, our brain has a different agenda. As alcohol arrives, our brain will try to restore hormone balances.

It will:
- Increase the production of GABA to counter the reduction.
- Increase the production of glutamate for the same reason.
- Reduce the production of dopamine.

In time, we will feel sober again.

The risk to our health is that our brain may adapt to alcohol. If we drink a glass of wine each day, the brain will become ready for it. Without our being aware of it, the brain will alter hormone levels in anticipation of the amount of alcohol we normally drink. As an autonomous organ, the brain has been silently removing our reward from drinking.

Without understanding why, we fight for our reward. We drink two glasses of wine each day. The greater we fight for our reward, the more we drink. Over time, we wrongly believe our tolerance level is building and our liver is gaining a tough constitution. This is why (and how) heavy drinkers can consume three bottles of vodka a day without showing any visible signs.

FALSE TOLERANCE
Because the brain is fighting back, heavy drinkers believe they have a high tolerance to alcohol. In truth, they can drink elevated levels of alcohol because the brain is

fighting back harder, not because they have a stronger liver. Suddenly, the liver will fail, without warning or pain.

For these people, high alcohol consumption heralded the end of their days.
- Peter Cook (57).
- Oliver Reed (61).
- Richard Burton (59).
- George Best (59).
- Charles Kennedy (55).
- Errol Flynn (50).
- Amy Whitehouse (27).

All these people left us before reaching retirement age. But we remember them fondly. The journey to alcohol dependency can be deceptive and slow.

The next day
After a night of heavy drinking, we feel jaded in the morning. Although most of the alcohol has gone from our bloodstream overnight, we still feel unsettled. Our hormonal levels, altered from last night's drinking, have not yet normalised. For the earlier part of the day, we remain over-stimulated.

To feel less jaded, we have a morning nip of alcohol. A heavy drinker falsely believes this is a cure. But the brain, hormones, and alcohol are once again in a false balance. The harm alcohol does will continue.

SIGNS OF HARM
Early signs of a poor relationship with alcohol:
- Frequently, we drink more than intended.
- The first drink of the day is becoming earlier.
- Our life partner comments on the quantity of alcohol consumed.
- We drink alcohol just to recover from the shakes.

- We spend more on alcohol than food.
- We defer eating; we prefer alcohol.

For the heavy drinker, there is a daily journey. The craving starts early, and it will feel like hunger. To resist drinking, they set a time each day for the first. However, a routine of watching the clock becomes part of the day. Though still jaded from yesterday, a single drink will restore their false well being. After pouring the first drink, the urge and craving to drink is satisfied.

SAFETY LEVELS

Alcohol, being a toxin, has no safe level. Just as there is no safe level for driving, flying, or climbing a ladder. Risk is inherent in all our actions. While no level is without risk, there is a low-risk level. And that low level is set by government advice.

We are told not to exceed fourteen units of alcohol per week. The government regards this limit as the right balance between risk and safety. But why has the government set the safety level at fourteen units?

There is evidence that if we consume fourteen units per week, our risk exposure is a one per cent chance of dying from alcohol-related diseases. This is the same level of risk as that of driving and having a road accident. The one per cent risk (fourteen units) is what the government believes, on our behalf, is acceptable.

And yet we are free to set our own safety level. If we are prepared to see a higher risk, then we do. But the nanny-state also tells us the more we drink, the shorter our life expectancy. The exact amount of the decrease is not yet fully researched.

In broad terms:
- Twenty units a week reduces life expectancy by six months
- Thirty units by eighteen months
- Forty units by four years
- Alcoholic, by twenty-four years.

Even with broad statistics such as these, to increase our time in retirement, we should ideally stay under fourteen units. Or abstain completely. The harm that alcohol inflicts is unseen. In the UK alone, 9,500 people die each year from alcohol misuse.

Heavy drinkers who have stopped drinking are happy with their new life choice. They feel energised. They awake refreshed each morning. Life is more enjoyable.

GAMBLING: THE BRAIN'S RESPONSE
While gambling can be a great source of entertainment, there is a risk of addiction. Especially for the bored retiree. For them, risking money and winning can become a new daily purpose.

After working life
Gambling can give new retirees a renewed sense of purpose after years of working. Beating the odds and winning is the new purpose. And as a winning chance draws near, the brain is flooded with a rush of adrenaline and dopamine. We feel good. The mix of adrenaline and the feel-good hormone dopamine give us a powerful buzz. When we win, the purpose of our risk and reward has been delivered. We reap the financial reward when we beat the odds.

The mix of gambling, alcohol, and boredom is not ideal in retirement. If we are bored, alcohol and a good win will help us forget our boredom. However, the pleasure and reward gained by winning are fleeting. Our boredom will soon return. Once again, we crave the next adrenaline and dopamine whizz. However, the next win must be larger to generate the same excitement.

Thus, a gambling addiction creeps in. There is a risk of falling into a cycle of seeking bigger rewards with bigger bets. Bigger rewards increase the thrill. Without self-control, increasing the size of our bets will steal savings and retirement funds. Unless the addiction is arrested, it is common for many to use all sources of money and credit to feed the addiction. The ease of online gambling can lead to addiction among bored retirees.

Losing streak
While a losing streak is common, it is frustrating. The luck has gone and sometimes anger can boil. Anger for the wasted money, and towards the casino. The fear of losing more causes anxiety. To ease the anxiety, we chase the loss with bigger bets. By placing a larger bet, we hope to win more. Enough to recover from the loss. And yet, the odds are never in our favour. We attempt to fix a losing streak with the same means.

And then - seemingly to save the day - there is another good win. Dopamine flows. Having turned the corner, our purpose is back on track. Once again, our gambling skills are improving. Or so we think.

The reality: the gambling industry is a business. They exist to make a profit from our losses. The house will always win.

TO STOP
It is difficult to overcome a gambling addiction. Like any other activity or substance that gnaws away inside, it takes time to break away from the habit. Have patience

and seek help from support networks. Set goals and celebrate victories. The further along the path of recovery you get, the easier it will become. You will become less reliant on gambling for reward and purpose. Especially if you find activities that provide these things.

To help moderate gambling, remember:
- Gambling is not a reliable money-making scheme.
- Never chase losses.
- Never play when upset.
- Balance the activity of gambling with hobbies and other activities.
- Gambling and alcohol do not mix well.

Just as alcohol will risk our health, gambling will steal our money.

CHAPTER 9

FINDING EXTRA FUNDS

IDEAS FOR WHEN MONEY IS TIGHT

QUICK READ

Money is more than just a token to spend in the supermarket. It serves as a store of value generated by our productive labour. Without this store of value, we would find it hard to fund retirement. But the value of our token requires universal trust. Trust that uses assets to underpin the token's value. An asset that will not devalue. Gold has been the bedrock of such trust for thousands of years. As far back as 600 BC. However, in the past forty years, economies have swapped to fiat money to support their currencies.

Our relationship with money is shaped by our early

childhood. But in later life, understanding our "money type" is the secret to a happy retirement. There is a challenge as we transition from earning and spending to just spending. We may fear spending too much and be anxious that our money will expire before we do. Finding a balance between preserving our money pot and enjoying life is essential. At its heart, money is a medium. It is not a source of eternal youth or the guarantor of happiness.

The state pension has been supporting the retired for over one hundred years. It was Germany (with a hidden agenda) that introduced the world's first state pension. It was a bold move. The aim was to entice the working population to re-elect the government. However, could it be afforded? With sleight of hand, the qualifying age was set just above average life expectancy.

With the desire to help the older non-worker, Germany's idea soon spread around the world. A state pension is supported by the contribution model - the working population pays into a central fund. From this fund, a state pension is paid. Today, with the contribution model in crisis, changes are being made.

Even if we receive a state and private pension, there can be unexpected financial challenges. Challenges that prompt the need for additional income. To boost our income, we have two key sources. Our productive labour and assets. Starting a business is one use of our time, but this path comes with many challenges. Assets such as intellectual property or the home can generate income. Most decide on the simple path. They resume work.

While returning to work is counter to the ethos of retirement, it is an option. For some, the motivation is not money but to escape retirement boredom. Statistics say that one in four of us will go back to work within five years solely for this reason. Finding work can be hard, however. We may need to resharpen our skills and may face ageism in the workplace. Unfortunately, ageism has become embedded in society and seen as normal by many who are older.

Money planning can help us avoid returning to the workplace. With a known level of income, we budget our spending. Half is used for the essentials, with a third towards hobbies and luxuries. Although it is recommended by financial planners that at least 20 per cent should be put away for emergencies. Understanding and managing our spending can do more than liberate us from money anxiety in retirement. We know what we can afford and how our money will last a lifetime.

(End of quick read)

THE EVOLUTION OF MONEY

While we use money to buy the things we want, the main purpose of money is to store value. With money, we create a store of value from our productive labour. Thus, without storing value (saving), many of us would not retire. The concept of money relies on trust for its success. Otherwise, the things we adopt to store value would become worthless.

Bartering

Bartering is the exchange of goods. It was our sole method of exchanging goods for many years. The chicken farmer could exchange a chicken for a loaf of bread. If the baker declined the chicken, the farmer would go without.

Money

To overcome the farmer's dilemma, we created a universal and trusted source of exchange — money. In its simplest form, money is a token. The farmer could trade his chicken for a token at the butcher's. With the token in his purse, he could revisit the baker and swap his token for bread. The baker could then visit the candlestick maker. Tokens (money) are therefore circular.

However, for money to work, each token needed to have a universally agreed value. And that value needed to be both trusted and stable.

Commodities became the first to represent money. The earliest known example is in China. Here, 6,000 years ago, people used salt as money. But in modern times, we use precious metals such as gold and silver.

Having money, and being able to store its value, has enabled us to hone our skills, achieve success in our job, and lead the life we want. We can store money for future use, for emergencies, and for times of hardship. When we are no longer reliant on our productive labour for money, we draw on our store for retirement.

Gold

Because gold is hard to mine, it is ideal as a stable commodity. With limited supply, the risk of flooding the economy with gold is low. Because of rarity, there is universal confidence that one ounce of gold will maintain its value.

Banks

As individual wealth grew, carrying an increasing weight of gold around became tiresome. If we left our gold unattended at home, theft was common. So, as a solution, we entrusted our gold to the goldsmith. The goldsmith would issue a receipt confirming the value held for safekeeping. Later, we could return, present the receipt, and reclaim our wealth.

Sometimes, returning to the goldsmith was not possible. It was easier, instead, to use our receipts to buy goods. We could do this because merchants trusted the goldsmiths. All receipts in circulation were equal to the value of gold held.

Thus, we saw the birth of two fundamentals that we see today:
 • The goldsmiths became an early banking facility.
 • Receipts became paper money.

Although the paper is worthless, the value is held in the vaults. Even today, sterling notes say: "I promise to pay the bearer on demand the sum of".

Fiat money
While gold is still used as the primary commodity, there is a lesser reliance. In 1971, President Nixon passed an act that introduced fiat money. Gold no longer supports the US dollar. From 1971, the dollar maintains its value by authority.

This authority comes from, for example:
- Central banks.
- Economic supply and demand.
- Government's political fancy (monetary policy).

By using fiat money, governments have flexibility when responding to changing economic conditions.

MONEY AND OUR LIFE
Understanding our money type will help us in retirement. But there have been past influences that affect our current attitudes to money (our money type).

Past influences
From the age of about seven, we begin to understand the concept of money. We see the emotions our parents have, and we learn what happens when money is scarce. Especially when asking for the things we crave. If we are denied these things, our younger mind feels hurt at being refused.

Unbeknown to us, our parents had other financial concerns. But it was these early denials that gave shape to our thoughts about money today. In adulthood, we view the lack of money with fear and anxiety. Therefore, we logically think that wealth will bring security and safety.

The common values that we attribute to money are:
- Security and comfort.

- Health and happiness.
- Enriching our retirement.
- Engaging with hobbies and activities.
- Helping others.
- Saving our labour and time.

To have the right relationship with money is one of our retirement challenges. Before we leave work, we are happy with our relationship with money. Earning and spending. However, this relationship will change when we retire. We will only be spending. For our retirement days, the ideal is to find a balance between our retention of money and our spending. But retirement will mean that we draw down (and depend upon) our lifetime's worth of savings. This may concern some.

DETACHMENT

The role of our bank account is to hold a level of commodity. A commodity to exchange for our needs. Depending on our financial aspirations, money should serve us before we leave this world.

But no amount of money will:
- Grant us eternal youth.
- Bring happiness (unless helping those less fortunate).
- Mend a broken relationship.
- Boost well-being and confidence.
- Help to find a perfect life-partner.
- Attract friends.

Money will never be part of you. Money in your pocket cares little if you are happy or successful. Sad or lonely. Or even dead or alive. In March 2021, a billionaire lost his life in a helicopter crash. His wealth could not preserve his skills and wisdom. His money, however, lives on.

MONEY PERSONALITIES

Our life experiences give us our money type. In retirement, how we use money will steer our lifestyle.

The compulsive earner

The compulsive earner will find it hard to retire. To feel secure, they work for the accumulation of money. They work beyond retirement age to keep a positive flow of money. If they stop working, they fear spending their savings.

The urge to keep a positive flow of money into savings can be an addictive behaviour. They feel a rush of satisfaction with increasing worth. By working hard, they believe having more will improve their status. For them, the path to happiness lies in the bank balance. However, before retirement age, they have devoted too many years to the saving cause. Having worked long and hard, there is the risk of neglecting health and relationships.

In the extreme, the stress of working hard to create wealth will lead to ill health. Becoming frail, the compulsive earner has little choice but to retire. Having worked long and hard, they have few close friends. Without the carefree days of later life, their money also fails to bring them happiness. The compulsive earner feels frustrated and disappointed.

The compulsive saver

A compulsive saver will put money aside for no purpose. Likewise, they will cut their spending on necessities. Purely for the sake of saving money. Saving (or not spending), helps them feel secure in their relationship with money. They are reducing the fear of having no money, even though their savings and pension income are sufficient.

Unless the plan is to transfer wealth after passing, we should aspire to find the right balance between saving and spending. By not spending and over-saving, we deprive ourselves of the happiness and freedoms retirement brings.

The worrier

With some merit, the worrier has a fear of losing their money. Either from lack of confidence when handling money, or from the worry that someone will defraud them. We can find a resolution by knowing what we can control. If we keep track of our finances and learn about the scams that plague us all, we can reduce our worries.

The consumer's association Which? has a free scam alert service at www.which.co.uk.

The compulsive spender

The compulsive spender will shop to relieve boredom. They love the buzz of the fresh and new. Spending brings positive emotions. Especially if they surround themselves with new clothes. The credit card is never far away. And the hidden advantage of a credit card is...? The pleasure of buying is separated from the pain of paying.

There are risks if we spend to relieve stress and boredom. The positive emotions we gain are often short-lived. Compulsive spending will end in buyer's remorse.

The compulsive comparisons

Society's norms can also shape our spending. Suggestions on what to aspire to are everywhere we look. Should we become unhappy with what we have, we feel compelled to remove feelings of inadequacy or jealousy. And we do so by spending beyond our means. Now money is controlling us. Our money pot is always wanting.

If money and status have a controlling influence, it is not a healthy relationship. Reflect on what we have rather than how we rank. There will always be those with higher pensions, bigger bank balances, or the latest red car. Pause and stop the comparisons.

The poor relationship
We do not have a poor relationship with money if we are finding it hard to cover basic living costs. During inflationary times, we call this the high cost of living. However, if we are spending beyond our means, we call this the cost of high living.

The healthy relationship
Unless we keep control of our money, money will be our master. It will rule our retirement with fear and anxiety. To regain control, we must change our habits and renew our relationship. Start by recording expenses. Over time, this will help you control your spending. By grouping expenses into categories, you can see patterns.

Whatever money type, you're going to want to :
- Stop using credit cards (unless essential).
- Stop shopping when bored.
- Stop buying on impulse.
- Stop buying for status.
- Stop spending to keep up with society.

But more than that: once you understand your spending pattern, you can build a simple budget (there's more detail on this later in the chapter). Remember to include provision to save for emergencies. A financial adviser might suggest putting away ten per cent of income. However, any debt should be reduced first.

At the end of the month, stay connected with your money. If you review your bank statements, you can understand trends and spot any odd transactions. Financial challenges are easier to manage, too, if you stay connected.

Partners
Within a relationship, there can be conflicting ideas on how to spend. Each will have desires and aspirations, but when money is tight, there are arguments. We may repeat these arguments, but they end without resolution. In the extreme, one partner may even conceal income or spending from the other.

When forming a fresh relationship, we sometimes find opposites attract. The saver is drawn to the spender as they discover how to enjoy life. Those who spend find the saver will offer money security. The attraction may not last, however. What gave birth to the relationship can ignite arguments.

Sudden wealth
Sudden wealth (while subjective) is still life-changing. But not always for the better. Few of us are prepared for the suddenness of a lottery win, for example. If we hope new wealth will fix our problems, it will not.

In the UK, two-thirds of big lottery winners are financially back to where they started within five years. Worse still, one-third declare themselves bankrupt. The principal causes for their downfalls are:
- Poor investments.
- Failed business ideas.
- Over-extravagant lifestyles.

Big wins will encourage many to leave working life. But they are unprepared for spending more time with their partner. Having more time together can cause relationship stress. Money, sadly, does not bring happiness to the floor of the divorce court.

Head in the sand
The sand-header does not save for retirement. This is not meant to be unkind, but there are those who lack understanding. Or perhaps there is too much focus on present-day needs. They believe the state pension will provide for them in later life.

In truth, the state pension (in the UK at least) will not provide. What we receive will depend on our National Insurance contributions record. But even with a full contribution record, the UK state pension will only give a basic living standard. Relying on the state pension to fund retirement life will cause hardship.

Thus, to fund cars, gifts, and holidays, those with their heads in the sand must work beyond retirement age. The dream of full-time retirement fades as they rely on working for income. There will come a time when their health and energy decline. And when they do, staying in the workplace will no longer be possible. They are forced to retire, ending their days reliant on state support. A sad scenario for sure. They have endured a lifetime of work and yet have deprived themselves of a glorious period of life, retirement.

Apart from that, a few individuals have particular reasons for not saving. Such as:
- A belief that they will never reach retirement age.
- Distrust of pension providers.
- A belief that a lottery win will help them when the time comes.

THE PENSION REVOLUTION

It was Germany that gave the world paid retirement, the state pension.

In 1889, Chancellor Otto von Bismarck announced a social security act that seemed too good to be true. Anyone over the age of sixty-five could claim a state pension. However, there were hidden reasons for such a bold offer.

It was to curry favour with the working class and win the next election. Initially, the government deemed the scheme too costly. But Bismarck had done his sums. By setting the qualifying age at sixty-five, he knew the cost to the state would be low. He knew life expectancy was sixty-two — three years short of the qualifying age. Even if someone reached sixty-five, few would live for that much longer.

Soon, the idea spread around the world. In 1935, a similar pension plan was presented to the American people. Given the same qualifying age (sixty-five), businesses were happy to adopt the new rules. They knew those in their sixties were slow and less efficient. Employing elders made their businesses less competitive.

With a retirement age of sixty-five enshrined in law, there was little to stop businesses from removing their older workers, leaving them free to recruit younger and faster people. Although this was good for businesses, the older worker had lost their retirement choice.

Around the world, the common retirement age of sixty-five was born.

THE CONTRIBUTION MODEL

The contribution model is simple to create. The working population pays into a pension fund. Those in retirement and entitled to it, draw a pension from the fund. In the UK, we know this as National Insurance.

At the start, the contribution model worked well. The working population during the 1930s outnumbered those in retirement. Each year, there was a comfortable surplus. And each year, funds in the national pension pot grew.

If we fast forward to the twenty-first century, however, the contribution model is showing signs of strain. The demand upon the pension pot is now double that when compared with its introduction. The surplus is now reversing.

Governments did not foresee this steep decline for two reasons:
- Between 1946 and 1964, the number of people born each year accelerated. This was thought to be triggered by the end of World War II; people born during these years are known as baby boomers. Sixty years later, these boomers are now retiring in vast numbers. The demand for pension payments is greater than the working population can contribute. Over the past two decades, the comfortable surplus has been falling.
- The second reason is simple. We are just living longer.

Anyone over sixty-five today has a greater chance of good health. Improved health has created a new life stage: the third age. In the UK, twelve million people (eighteen per cent of the population) are over sixty-five.

In response to the funding crises, many governments are now increasing the state retirement age. If they continue with the same level of support from declining funds, the reserve will run dry. The ratio of workers to non-workers is the reverse of what it was when Bismarck's idea was conceived. Change is needed.

Trouble in France
In recent years, France has looked to increase its retirement age. But the move was met with widespread opposition. Many parts of society saw the change as unfair to the working class. Everyone should have access to a dignified retirement, they felt.

UK PENSIONS

State Pension
Following the adoption of the Old Age Pensions Act 1908, the first state pension was paid in January 1909. But the conditions to qualify were much harsher than today's requirements. To claim, the qualifying age was seventy. And you had to be of moral character. Given only five per cent of the population reached seventy, the burden on the public purse was always going to be low.

To receive a full state pension today, a full National Insurance contribution record is required. But even then, a full pension will still provide only a low living standard. It is just enough to meet the basic needs of food and shelter. Few luxuries can be afforded. State pensions are proportionately lower for those with a contribution record of between ten and thirty-five years.

It is estimated that ten per cent of the UK population have the state pension as their main source of income. A happy retirement may be hard for anyone subsisting on a state pension.

Today, the UK state retirement age is increasing to sixty-eight. Despite concerns, the UK has not witnessed the level of protests seen in France over the change. However, because the change was introduced with such short notice, there have been several legal challenges.

Review your entitlement
You can review your pension forecast on the HMRC website: www.gov.uk/check-state-pension. You will need a Government Gateway account first. Applying is easy, though setting it up takes time.

While the state pension cannot exceed the maximum payment each year, you can increase your state pension by deferring it. If you choose to delay your entitlement for a year, you will receive a slightly higher amount. However, not by much. Having deferred for a year, it may take fifteen years to break-even. Thus, deferment has a marginal advantage.

For every nine weeks you choose not to receive your entitlement, the state pension will increase by one per cent. If you delay the right to claim by fifty-two weeks, the increase will be 5.8 per cent. And it will remain at this higher rate for the rest of your days. While this increase may seem generous, the government is hedging its bets.

For example, retire at sixty-seven with a state pension of £180 per week. Given life expectancy is eighty-two, you could draw the state pension for the next sixteen years:

- No deferment: receive £181,399 over sixteen years.
- Deferred a year: receive £182,017 over fifteen years.

By electing not to receive £9,360 in the first year, you gain an extra benefit of just £618 over the fifteen years. And that benefit does not arrive until your eighty-second birthday. Is there any coincidence that this is also our life expectancy?

The future of state pension
While we are living longer, we also see birth rates falling. The working population (which contributes to the public purse) is reducing, too. As more baby boomers retire and claim the state pension, the fund is coming under increasing strain. To relieve the strain, governments worldwide must make unpopular changes.

One such change is to increase the qualifying age. Until 2010, a woman in the UK could claim entitlement at sixty, a man at sixty-five. Since 2020, both men and women need to reach sixty-seven to claim.

The OBR (Office for Budget Responsibility) predicts that by the year 2040, a one-year increase in the qualifying age will save £10 billion each year. To reduce the pension burden even more, there is speculation that the government may means-test our entitlement.

HOW MUCH INCOME IS NEEDED
What income is necessary for retirement? This is a good question and a common one. You can make a rough estimate by calculating three numbers based on your pre-retirement income. If your pre-retirement income is £2,500 per month, you need to find three values:

A: — One half of the pre-retirement income.
B: — Three quarters of the pre-retirement income.
C: — The average of A & B

Answers:
A = £1,250 (1/2).
B = £1,875 (3/4).
C = £1,562 (average).

Assuming your lifestyle remains consistent post-retirement, your required income will be:
A: — Not less than £1,250
B: — At most £1,875
C: — But, on average, £1,562.

While this is a rough measure, it does at least allow a starting point for money planning. Planning, however, will always have an element of guesswork.

As part of that planning, you may find in retirement you are spending less on:
- Commuting.
- Workplace clothing.
- Mortgage repayments (if any)
- Dependent children (who have become independent adults).
- Status symbols (which may have less importance).
- And of course, pension contributions.

We cover money planning in a later chapter. However, let us briefly explore the money landscape for the year ahead.

Using the average from the example above, our annual income need is £18,744. Knowing that our annual state pension will be £12,000 (roughly), we can already see a shortfall of £6,744 each year. With this revelation, we can boost our income with equity release, part-time work, or allowing our savings to drain.

INCOME TYPES

PRIVATE PENSIONS
It is said that paying into a pension is the ultimate delayed reward. We pay into a pension knowing there is performance risk too. And yet, we do. There are two types of private pension. The defined benefit and the defined contribution.

Defined benefit pension
This type of pension is ideal for the retiree, but rarely seen these days. The pension entitlement is defined by the scheme rules and the pension you will receive is based upon your final salary. Better yet, the pension fund is protected from poor management or performance. If the pension fund falls short, the employer must cover the gap. For the retiree, you are guaranteed an agreed level of pension when you retire.

Defined contribution pension
With this type of pension, the amount you pay into the scheme is a set amount. How much you receive back is governed by the fund's performance and management. At retirement, the investment is cashed and buys a regular pension income. These schemes are run by pension providers, not the employer. If the employer becomes insolvent, the pension fund remains protected. The employer is no longer at risk should the fund under-perform.

Some factors that influence the final retirement pot are:
- The level of contributions.
- The fees taken by the pension provider.
- The quality of fund management.

According to a recent estimate by the bank HSBC, the average retirement fund is a mere £30,000. Someone retiring at sixty-seven would expect to receive just £1,400 each year with a fund this low. This leaves them reliant on a state pension for retirement funding.

Risk
Today, pension funds are usually risk free and will provide when retirement arrives. However, it was not always this way. In the 1980s, the owner of the Mirror group plundered the company's pension fund to support their struggling business. The fund collapsed, leaving thousands of retirees without a pension.

At the turn of the century, Equitable Life came close to collapse as well. While these were darker times for the pension industry, pension schemes are now protected by tough laws and regulations.

ALTERNATIVES

Financial Independence Retire Early movement.
The FIRE movement began in the early 1990s - a life-style choice that follows a hard path to early retirement. Followers of FIRE say the traditional way our retirement is funded is flawed. By allowing pension providers to manage their money, they had no control over their eventual retirement funds. To them, it was playing a game of Russian roulette.

Instead, devotees of FIRE build passive incomes - an income that flows from an asset. Writing is one example. After the author has crafted their book, it becomes an asset. It will generate an income without further time and skill (in theory).

Even in retirement, there are ways to join the FIRE movement. Popular ideas include:
- Building savings to pay interest.

- Property rental.
- Creating a YouTube channel with interesting content.
- Developing online training courses.
- Photographic and artwork royalties.
- Automated drop-shipping.
- Share portfolio investment.
- Stock market trading.
- And lastly, writing a novel.

The FIRE movement is popular with Millennials and Generation Z. (those born between 1981 and 2012). These two generations are more adaptive and open to change than today's baby boomers (1946 to 1964) and Generation X (1965 to 1980).

NEEDING MORE INCOME
Even with the best prepared retirement plans, we can still face the unexpected. If we need to boost our income, what options do we have? Income can flow from two central sources: either from our productive labour or from an asset. Assets can include intellectual property, such as art, music, or writing.

Productive labour
Using your productive labour will mean returning to work or starting a business. Going back to work goes against the retirement ethos, but it remains an option.

Running a business can be fun and rewarding. However, there is more to a business than just being an expert at what the business produces. You must wear many hats and most of those hats will be unfamiliar.

We might struggle with bookkeeping. Or shudder at employing people. We must connect with customers, deal with suppliers, and suffer the burden of red-tape. And then, there is no guarantee that our efforts will generate a profit.

There are pleasures when empire building, however. We are free to follow our vision. With creative control, we can shape our "creative window", a business that best serves the customer above all others. We may even enjoy building relationships that become a blend of business and personal life.

ASSETS

Demand is needed for an asset to generate income. It needs to be something people are willing to pay for. For example, Leo Tolstoy created his own intellectual property by writing War and Peace. But there would be little income from it if only a few people wanted to read this lengthy epic.

The family home can be our biggest asset. Therefore, we can also boost income by:
- Taking a lodger.
- Downsizing to a smaller home.
- Extracting cash from its value (equity release).

These are all emotive choices, but they are options to boost income.

TAKING A LODGER

Sharing your living space with a stranger will have elements of concern. This is normal for both you (as landlord) and the lodger. And yet, if we prepare and ready ourselves, it can work.

Before meeting the lodger, here are a few things to check first:

- If you rent your home, review the tenancy agreement.
- If your home secures a loan, tell the lender. If possible, ask for written confirmation.
- Check your insurances. Some policies exclude damage caused by those entitled to be on the property.

First meeting

Usually, the first meeting takes place later in the day. It should be open and friendly. A chance to meet them without obligation. Likewise, the potential lodger wants to feel relaxed in their potential accommodation. They want to understand what you have to offer, what is excluded, and, most of all, to meet you.

While this is an informal meeting, there are important questions to ask:

- What working hours do they keep? Will working nights be a problem? Will it be frustrating to have to remain silent during the day?
- When would they use the kitchen?
- Would they need any dietary variations in the kitchen?
- What belongings would they bring, and how much?
- If they have a partner, would you allow them to stay overnight?
- Is there a reason they prefer lodging over finding their own place? This may give an insight into their current circumstances.
- Have they shared a house before, and why did they leave?
- Do they smoke or vape? If they smoke but promise to quit, have doubts. What would you do

if they lean out the window for a sneaky drag?
- Ask for references, proof of income and confirmation of ID. If they decline, is this a warning?

Ask yourself
- Could I live with this person?
- Do I find their traits grating or annoying?
- Do they seem respectful?
- Do they seem hygienic?
- Is their lifestyle compatible with mine?

While all the above may seem clinical, you and your lodger both want a private life. However, you and they will share common rooms such as the kitchen or bathroom. In the kitchen, meat eaters and vegetarians may have conflicts. While the pull of money is important, be honest with yourself. Is the arrangement ideal?

Lodger agreements
A lodger agreement will set out expectations both ways. Clarifying what is included and excluded in the rent. Do not rely on a verbal agreement. It is human nature to remember only what we want to hear. While a verbal agreement might keep the arrangement friendly, in the longer term, a written and signed agreement will help avoid arguments.

Here are a few suggested terms:
- The amount of rent, and when the lodger pays.
- The deposit amount.
- What the lodging includes and excludes. For example, the lodging might include light, heat, and water, but not food, laundry, and the telephone.
- Say which areas are out of bounds. Rooms where you can enjoy your own company.

- Their room (and shared rooms) are to be kept clean and tidy.
- Is the lodging open-ended or for a set term?
- Allow a reasonable notice period to end the lodging.
- When they leave, what are the procedures?
- Will you allow an open house or have boundaries with over-night guests?

Prepare a list of furnishings, together with a note of their condition. At the end of the lodging, consider fair wear and tear and how they will compensate for any damage. Photographing carpets, doors, windows, bed, and light fittings will help.

Taxation
In the UK, the first £7,500 of lodging income is tax-free. Known as "The Rent a Room scheme", this tax-free status has several qualifying conditions:
- The lodging must be part of your home, not an annex.
- You must live in the same home.
- Furnishing must be provided.

While the first £7,500 of lodging income is tax-free, social benefits may be affected — including the single person council tax reduction. If the annual lodging income is over £7,500, inform HMRC and complete a tax return.

Within this return, you have a declaration of choice:
- Declare all rents and deduct those expenses incurred to provide the accommodation. You will pay tax on this amount.
- Or claim no expenses and pay tax on every £1 above £7,500.

DOWNSIZING

Moving to a smaller home can provide a boost to savings. Assuming that the smaller home is cheaper, we release equity tied up in the larger property.

In the UK, selling the family home and making a "profit" is tax-free. To qualify for this PRR (private residence relief), the property must not be a holiday cottage or a second home. Only the main residential property can qualify for this tax-free status. Take advice when selling a second property. There may be opportunities to save tax.

Also consider these downsizing costs:
- Agency and legal fees for selling.
- Stamp duty.
- Modifications needed after buying.
- Moving cost and replacing damaged items.
- Storage for excess furniture/personal memorabilia.

The family home

Selling the family home has an emotional cost, too. Over the years, it has been a haven for safety and comfort. Our family gathers under this roof as we celebrate festivals and exchange stories. The family home is a unique place.

Inside the home, there are items that preserve those memories. Removing these will bring apprehension. With a smaller property, we worry about excluding our adult children. We question whether they will call or stay over.

For adult children, the family home will always be a special place. However, since leaving home, they will have developed their own traditions and celebrations. They will encourage you to join them. The family bond will remain after downsizing. It has just moved to a new place.

Declutter

While living in a smaller home will reduce running costs, a smaller space will have challenges. Around the home there are mementos and souvenirs that help you re-imagine experiences. These things give shape and meaning to our home. And, naturally, you elevate these things to a level of special importance.

The challenge is to squeeze these mementos and souvenirs into a smaller space. But sometimes this is far from easy. One solution is to create a vision for the new home. Making life easier in small property is the goal.

To begin the declutter, have two boxes ready. Mark one box "for keeping" and the other "for disposal". Have the resolve to declutter. Step into a room used daily. Scan the space and start with the smaller items first. Progress with smaller things will drive your determination to stay on track.

Feeling overwhelmed? Start with a notebook. Break the task down into manageable parts. Head each page with a room name. Underneath, note down any essential items. What remains can be disposed of. Break down the house into individual rooms and treat them as mini projects.

And yet, your resolve may still weaken. Hesitation arises when unsure. Being unsure will cause uneasiness and stop the process. A solution is to be quick about your decisions. However, you may feel the urge to begin a third box. A "maybe keep" box. If you do this, your thinking will slow again and then stop altogether. Instead, photograph the item (as a memory keepsake) and head towards the disposal box.

What to do with the disposal box
Here are some suggestions for the contents:
- Invite the family over. Is there anything special they want to keep?
- Invite neighbours to buy.
- Sell at a boot sale.
- Use social media, saying "collect for free".
- There are charities that collect larger items of furniture. While there is little or no cost, the fire-resistant label must be present.

Advantages of downsizing
- Cheaper than equity release schemes.
- Lower utility bills.
- Less maintenance and upkeep.
- Can move to a preferred location.
- Have a home better suited to physical needs.

Disadvantages of downsizing
- Less space which causes stress.
- No escape room for quiet downtime.
- Fewer or no guest bedrooms.

Renting first
Before downsizing, there is a growing trend to rent a smaller home first. We can explore various locations before becoming settled. But there are drawbacks.

The lack of permanency may be concerning. At the end of the rental term, the landlord may ask you to leave the property. You may face rent increases and repairs that you cannot control. That said, renting first and keeping the family home has two financial benefits. Larger equity gain and rental income.

By keeping the family home, we have a bigger equity gain when compared to a smaller property. On average, property values increase by 10 per cent each year. Compare these two scenarios.

- [A] Family home £650,000 plus 10% = gain £65,000
- [B] Smaller home bought for £400,000 plus 10% = gain £40,000.

Had we sold the family home and downsized to a smaller property, we would have bypassed an equity gain of £25,000. While property values will fluctuate over a five-year period, we may have lost over £100,000 by downsizing. An amount that could have been available using an equity release scheme.

Renting the family home
Rent from the family home can fund the smaller property. However, you need to be happy with strangers living there. Depending on your personal tax position, rental income may have a tax burden. Most accountants can help with tax returns and payments.

Cash flow working example:
A: — Rent from the larger property of £2,000.
B: — Basic rate UK tax @ 20% of £400.
Gives £1,600 (A less B).
Rent for smaller home £1,500.
Leaving £100 each month as a small boost to retirement income.

EQUITY RELEASE
Another growing trend is to extract funds from the value of your home. Equity release transforms a slice of the home into tax-free cash. Thus, you can avoid downsizing and having to declutter. You control property ownership

and may live there. The property is sold when the last resident passes or enters long-term care. While popular, equity release schemes have a high cost. More so than a standard mortgage lending.

In simple terms, an equity release is a loan arrangement based on the value of your home. A value calculated by market forces and other loans secured on it.

As a simple example:
- Property with a market value of £500,000.
- Less outstanding mortgage of £200,000.
- Net equity of £300,000.

Few providers (if any) will lend 100 per cent of the equity. Lending rates vary between 20 per cent and 80 per cent depending on the type of arrangement used. The rules governing the scheme will repay the borrowing. Equity release is a growing market that will boost your pension savings. But always clearly understand the terms. Leaving an equity release scheme early can be costly.

The schemes outlined here are to create awareness only. This does not give financial advice. There are two popular equity release schemes: lifetime mortgages and home reversion.

Lifetime mortgages
In 2020, the Equity Release Council reported that 99 per cent of schemes were lifetime mortgage arrangements. These arrangements are akin to an interest-only mortgage — a type of mortgage where repayment of the original loan is requested at the end of the term. The term ends when the last resident enters long-term care or passes away. The scheme provider will then sell the home to repay the amount borrowed, plus interest.

Advantages
- No test for affordability because lending is based on the property's value.
- No monthly payments are needed. Although with some schemes you have the option to pay interest each month.
- To safeguard family inheritance, you can hold part of the property's value outside the scheme.
- You can receive a one-time lump-sum payment or a monthly income.

Disadvantages
- Interest rates can be high and remain fixed throughout the agreement.
- Compound interest. Avoid this by selecting a scheme that allows the payment of interest.
- A lump sum can affect means-tested benefits.
- A lifetime mortgage is a lifelong commitment.
- Leaving the scheme may not be possible.

Home reversion
Home reversion arrangements are less common and have a higher qualifying age than lifetime mortgages.

The equity provider will buy and own part of the home to give you a lump sum. While the home is under split ownership, you can stay in the property rent-free. This quasi tenancy will end when the last resident enters long-term care or passes away. The equity provider will sell the home and divide the proceeds between them and your estate.

To use the scheme, the provider will value the home at under market value. They then give you a percentage lump sum based on this lower value. When sold, to calculate the equity providers' share, they apply the same percentage to the full sale price. Or to put it another way:

- They buy a share of the home at under market price.
- When sold, they receive a share at the market rate.

If we compare this scheme with a lifetime arrangement, home reversion has a lesser cost. However, this is only true if property prices stay unchanged over the term. That not being likely, home reversion schemes are poor value for money.

Retirement mortgages

This type of mortgage is becoming popular with those in retirement. We know them as retirement interest-only mortgages without a fixed-term date. While we pay the monthly interest, we settle the mortgage after we pass or enter long-term care. This avoids compound interest.

- You keep 100 per cent of the home.
- It has no fixed term, but it ends when the last resident moves into long-term care or passes away. Thereafter, the lender may repossess and sell the property to repay the mortgage.
- There is no upper qualifying age limit, but lenders will set their own maximum application age.
- A typical lender may offer 8.5 times the annual income.

The legacy question

While these schemes can give a much-needed cash boost in later life, our financial legacy will be lower. Should we therefore ask ourselves: Is it fair to spend freely during our best years or should we save for our children's future?

There are no right or wrong answers here, since it is subjective. Those in favour of "skiing", (Spending the Kids' Inheritance) might say:

"After decades of hard work and careful saving, I want to experience retirement life to the fullest. My money is to be enjoyed, not a nest egg for our children."

Some financial advisers now recommend a retirement plan that leaves no legacy.

RETURNING TO WORK
It was previously suggested that a return to work was a way to increase income. But money is not always the main motivation.

As we have seen, it is estimated that one in four will return to work within five years to ease their boredom. To rekindle their purpose and feel less isolated. Without purpose and social connection, they return to work to feel valued again.

When back in the workplace, they find:
- Their career passion is reborn.
- Their mind is kept active.
- They have identity and value again.
- Their day has structure and purpose.

Returning to the workplace is not retirement failure. You can reset and try again when ready.

Finding work
Finding work may be a struggle, despite our determination. We may need work, but work does not need us. We may have fallen behind with technology, and our working methods are now outdated. As a result, our skills are no longer needed or relevant. We should lower our salary expectations, too. And perhaps what shocks us most, we will be managed by someone younger. However, despite these drawbacks, we still have plenty to offer.

Being visible is the first step to finding work. Speak to past work colleagues, create a LinkedIn profile, use agencies, or contact businesses of interest. Have a natural e-mail address and voice mail message. Anything outlandish can harm your chances. Check your publicly accessible media, such as Facebook or Instagram. Review your settings and images. Whether you like it or not, open social media can influence your success rate.

Employment agencies
Employment agencies are great for job seekers. They often have working relationships with many businesses and will understand their needs. They have the expertise to pair us with the perfect employer. But they are not your only source.

For lower-skilled work, employers will use online job boards first, because they are cheaper. Plus, online job boards allow them to ask pre-interview questions to improve the quality of applicants. Most questions demand a yes or no answer, but beware of traps.

Employers know some applicants are lazy. They answer yes to all options, not aware that one asks, "I confirm I have read this question by ticking no." Anyone ticking yes has fallen at the first fence. Employers look for diligent applicants.

Steps for work
At every stage, you will connect with someone. One connection might be fleeting, another longer and involved. All these contact points will leave impressions. How you write, how you talk, or how you hold yourself. Connecting with others is essential to the working world. Leaving someone with a poor impression will harm your chances of securing work. Therefore, to increase your

success rate, make each connection count.

Your goal, in this job search quest, is to be sitting opposite the recruiter. Without connecting with someone across the interview table, your chances of finding work are slim.

Before making your first approach, understand what the business does. Nothing will damage your chances of success more than not knowing what happens in their industry.

Ask yourself what skills, strengths, and capabilities make you suitable for the role. And ensure it clearly says those things in your resume or CV. A resume is a one-page summary that is quick to read. A CV is a concise statement, not exceeding two pages. Going beyond this length increases the chance of the recruiter skim-reading after the first page.

CV hints
- Be clear, with consistent formatting.
- Summarise each past employment.
- Avoid jargon and abbreviations.

Common errors
- Spelling errors and poor grammar.
- Making the CV too long or verbose.
- Wrong contact information.
- Over-stating skills.
- Focusing on duties rather than achievements.
- Leaving out hobbies and interests.
- Unexplained gaps in employment history.
- Not explaining a sequence of short-term work.

Be sure to explain any gaps between employments. Gaps are often associated with struggles to find work. Likewise, a sequence of short-term work might suggest you are a problem employee.

Beware lack of originality
It is common to read the same phrases in multiple CVs. So much so, for the recruiter, they become overused and meaningless. For example:
- I am a hard worker.
- A quick learner.
- A good timekeeper.
- I am versatile and can work alone or as part of a team.

Worse still, "I play close attention to detail" followed by bad presentation, poor grammar, and other spelling mistakes (did you spot the error in "play"?).

If you use worn-out phrases, your CV is bland. Your CV is a special moment to highlight your qualifications and experiences.

Photograph
Including your photograph on a CV has both advocates and opponents. Advocates say few applications will include an image. Thus, a photo will enhance the CV. As we all connect with people, a photograph will show our personal side. But choose a picture that is current and professional. Not a holiday snap drinking outside Harry's Bar in Corfu. Those who oppose say our application can be rejected solely based on appearance.

Covering letter
A covering letter is your chance to add personality. While a CV can be dry and factual, your covering letter should capture their attention. Use words and phrases that express eagerness to join their company.

Such as:
- I am excited about...
- I am eager to use my skills...
- I have a passion for...

Include words that convey genuine enthusiasm for the role. Say why you are applying and your long-term intentions. Look for ways to solve their problems. How your lifelong career and professional development can help them.

The employer's perception of us can be important. If they say we are overqualified and will be bored in the role, suggest becoming a mentor to their younger employees. Be a star team member.

Despite laws to prevent age discrimination, you can still find resistance. While employers may (or may not) ask for your date of birth, you should not lie about your age. The best defence to counter this bias is to turn their focus onto your ability, not age.

Common errors
- Using a template letter.
- Addressing a different company.
- Restating the CV.
- False statements.

After submitting your application, do not chase for a response. Those tasked with recruiting balance the role with their day-to-day job. Disturbing them, and their work, may backfire. Instead, go to related trade shows, read news feeds, learn what is new in the industry. Knowing the latest developments can impress (if not surprise) some employers.

THE INTERVIEW

This is your chance to shine. You will feel excited, nervous, and hopeful. Reaching the interview stage should boost your confidence, but what should you do next? Being prepared for the interview is key to your success. Be ready to answer the common questions.

Among them will be:
- Tell me about yourself?
- Tell me why you applied for this position?
- What are your strengths and weaknesses?
- Give an example of where you have resolved a problem at work?

Be prepared also for the trendy "outside the box" questions, including:
- What animal would you be, and why?
- How many sheep are there in Australia?
- Explain Wi-Fi to your grandmother.

The answer is not important. These questions require you to think quickly and find answers. It is how you arrive at your answer that is significant.

Body language

Your body language can be just as important as what you say. By making eye contact, you can appear confident and engaged. Sit up straight and avoid crossing your arms. Stay cautious if you are not enthusiastic about going back to work. Your body language can send powerful unintended messages.

During the interview

You will feel your character is under scrutiny. Not the knowledge and insight you can bring to the company. Employers have a broader perspective. They ask, would you bond with the current team? Would you be disruptive? Your success at finding a job can simply be about whether they like you.

Keep in mind
The interviewer may be younger and have less experience than you. If they appear to be nervous, they are.
- Let them steer the interview.
- Ask the right questions (see below).
- Avoid the wrong questions (see below).
- Listen well. Silently repeat the question and stay on the subject.

Right questions
- How would I carry out my role? This question shows we are ready for any training.
- What would be a typical day? The job description will cover the basics and what the responsibilities are. This question digs a little deeper. For example, would I be working alone or as part of a team?
- What makes the role enjoyable? This should invite a personal insight.
- Does the company encourage social activity?
- What would the ideal candidate expect to achieve in the first six months? Beware of a vague answer. The role might contribute little to the team, not be valued, or be stressful.
- Does the company encourage new ideas from the team? If not, is there a culture of arrogance to avoid?

Wrong questions
- Asking what the company does is not a good idea: the answers can be easily found with basic research.
- Don't ask too many questions about what the company can offer, instead of focusing on what

you can contribute.
- Do not ask the interviewer personal questions.
- Do not ask the interviewer what they dislike about the company.
- Avoid repeating a question.
- Don't refuse to answer important and reasonable questions.

OUR SPENDING TYPES

Knowing what we spend (and where we spend) is part of our retirement responsibility. If we understand our spending, we have a framework around which we can avoid money anxieties. Including the stress of having to return to work.

There are three kinds of spending. Things we buy that are essential. Spending that is discretionary. And putting money aside for the unexpected.

The general rule says:
- 50 per cent of monthly income is for essential spending.
- 30 per cent for discretionary.
- 20 per cent for the unexpected.

While this rule is rough "n" ready, it does at least allow somewhere to start our planning.

Essential

To safeguard our health, we spend on the essentials of life. And yet, what we buy is also in keeping with our lifestyle. Spending on essentials is in keeping with our expectations. As we read in the happiness section, meeting our lifestyle expectations will keep us happy.

The essentials of life will include:
- Maintaining a home.
- Transport.

- Food, drink, and medical.
- Connectivity.
- Hobbies and interests.
- Debt commitments.

Discretionary

This spending adds spice to our retirement. We buy the things we want, rather than what we need. Those things that are beyond our basic needs. For example, starting a new hobby, or treating ourselves to a special holiday.

But sometimes we overspend, such as:
- Redecorating the home on the whims of fashion.
- Taking frequent long-distance holidays.
- Overspending on impulse.
- Enjoying too many five-star restaurants.
- Buying the latest gadget for status.

In times of financial constraint, discretionary spending is the first to go.

Unexpected

Planning for the unexpected is harder to accommodate into any money budget. However, we can prepare for financial emergencies by saving. The recommended guide is the rule of 50/30/20 (as shown above): put aside 20 per cent of income to meet the unexpected.

Finding the data

Discovering your spending habits can be labour intensive. However, if most of your spending is cashless, your online bank statement will be a time saver. Just export your transactions as a CSV file, open it in Excel and use the "sort" command.

SPENDING ON DEBT

Starting retirement debt-free is the best way to begin a new chapter in life. From the first day, no one will make demands on your income or savings. You have complete control over your money.

However, there are a growing number of retirees who carry debt into their retirement life. For each £1,000 of debt, they owe:

- £500 to a credit card.
- £300 to unsecured loans.
- £150 towards the remains of their mortgage.

If the ratio of debt to income is high, advisers say to stay at work to reduce debt first. It decreases the likelihood of defaulting and being obliged to return to work.

Good debt
A good debt is where there is a positive association with our financial commitments. A loan that is put to a good purpose. A business loan or borrowing for a personal vision.

Bad debt
A bad debt arises from wasteful spending. Usually when we spend with little self-control. And yet, our emotions play a big role when we are impulsive. We use shopping to relieve negative feelings. We spend for the buzz but have buyer's remorse later. Strategies to avoid impulsive spending ask us to pause and reflect beforehand.

A debt could be bad when spending beyond our means. Buying a car for status, rather than functionality, is common and will strain our finances, for example.

BE THE MASTER OF MONEY

To be the master of your retirement funds, you need to plan your money. Money planning serves to defend your savings and deter you from overspending. You can bring knowledge of your future financial standing into the present day. Knowing how your savings will fare in two years' time eases anxiety over money. With an element of spending control, your retirement money should then last a lifetime.

Planning will help you to:
- Avoid limiting your activities because you fear running out.
- See how your fixed income will cover expenses.
- Make spending decisions.
- Plan for emergencies.

Creating a plan for our money today will help us enjoy a fuller retirement life. We no longer deny ourselves activities because we believe our money will not last. Other people, however, want to spend, spend, spend, just to avoid being the richest person in the graveyard.

A simple plan

In its purest form, a plan is simple mathematics. We start with a balance, add income, less spending, to give a closing balance. That closing balance becomes the opening sum for the next period. A period can be a week, month, or year. Whatever feels comfortable.

Working example

Starting with savings of £5,000, we have a fixed income of £2,000 per month. The predicted monthly spend is £2,100.

Month 1
Opening balance £5,000
Plus fixed income £2,000
Less predicted spend £2,100
Closing balance £4,900

Month 2
Opening balance £4,900
Plus fixed income £2,000
Less predicted spend £2,100
Closing balance £4,800

In this working example, we can see that savings are falling by £100 each month. Not a significant amount or a fast decline, but without planning may have gone unnoticed until in the advanced stage.

Planning
Our planning therefore begins with a known level of monthly income. We then apply the 50/30/20 rule we saw in the previous section and adjust our spending to fit.

This rough rule divides our income into three categories:
- 50 per cent for essential spending.
- 30 per cent for discretionary.
- 20 per cent towards emergencies (savings).

Applying the rule to a fixed income of £2,000, we have:
- £1,000 for essential spending.
- £600 for discretionary.
- £400 towards emergencies (savings).

This suggests we should reduce our spending to £1,600 per month, putting £400 into savings. This is a hard change, and yet needed for long-term saving stability. If we do not change our spending today, in five years' time our savings of £5,000 will have gone.

If the unexpected happens and we need to spend £6,000 on house repairs, a loan might be needed. Without planning, there would now be a loan making extra demands on our income.

Don't aim for precision when planning. Trying for accuracy will not serve a purpose and invites frustration. You will never perfectly align the future of what you spend and save to any plan. The aim of planning is to navigate a path along which you can balance the desire for a happy retirement and keep a savings pot. You may not refer to your plan very often, but you feel connected to your retirement savings.

HOMEWORK
- Gather data on income and spending.
- Create a monthly, one-year plan.
- Extend that to five years.
- Think about forthcoming big spends - put these costs into the plan.
- Consider any tax burden.

Partner harmony
If we share a spending plan with our partner, we will create harmony. Or at least avoid arguments over spending. A 2005 study found that married couples increased their joint wealth faster than single people. But in marriage, arguments over money are one predictor of divorce.

TAX BURDEN
Knowing how much tax we need to pay should also be part of money planning. After working life, paying tax remains a burden and a personal responsibility. While our private pension provider will deduct tax at source (if needed), we should review our income for the tax year.

In the UK, when our income within a tax year is above a certain threshold, the amount above the threshold is taxable. Anything below is tax-free (often called the tax-free allowance). The allowance is currently £12,570 per tax year, but it increases with each budget.

Common sources of income in retirement are:
- Private pension (before tax).
- Part-time work.
- Rental income.
- Savings interest.

It is a misconception in the UK that the state pension is tax free. State pension is only tax free when it is your only income - and below the tax-free allowance. Which, in most cases, if it is your only income, it will be.

Any form of income and state pension together may have tax implications. Consider Mr. A who retires early with a private pension of £11,000. Since this pension falls below the tax threshold, HMRC (the government body tasked with collecting tax) is not expecting any tax.

However, when he becomes entitled to the state pension, he receives an additional income of £9,400 per year. Now, Mr. A is receiving a total income of £20,400 each year, £7,830 above the tax-free threshold.

After HMRC introduced self-assessment in 1996, the duty to complete a tax return and pay tax lies with the individual. Hence the name, self-assessment. There is no requirement (in law) that says that HMRC must ask for tax.

But even if they don't ask, we are not free to avoid paying. Because the focus of the tax system is on self-assessing. Penalties cannot be avoided through ignorance. That said, HMRC will try to help and predict any tax liabilities. Should they believe tax is not reaching the public purse, they will issue a tax return. However, HMRC (His Majesty's Revenue and Customs) is slow to react.

In this age of electronic connectivity, HMRC has many sources of data. Data that is linked to individual taxpayers. Therefore, if you are sent a tax return to complete, do not ignore or forget it. There are fines for late submission.

HMRC data sources include
- Employers and pension providers.
- Banks, building societies, and other financial institutions.
- Government agencies, such as the Land Registry and council records.

To complete the example for Mr. A, his tax burden is calculated with the base rate. Base rate is currently 20 per cent, giving him a tax bill of £1,566. If Mr. A believed his state pension was tax free, this might come as a surprise.

Note that we receive a state pension every four weeks, instead of monthly. So Mr. A will receive thirteen payments each year, not twelve.

Most accountants can help with tax returns. However, regardless of their qualifications, ask who will do the work. Sometimes, especially in larger firms, they might assign bread "n" butter tax work to someone at a junior level.

SAVINGS

In the early days of retirement, our employer may reward us with a golden handshake or, if we are a UK resident, we may choose to take a lump sum from our pension pot.

As a result, having more money in our bank account than we are used to, we are at risk of rewarding ourselves with impulsive spending. Thus, be forever watchful for the media machine that begs us to buy.

Banks now recommend moving a high current account balance to a savings account. Mainly because of the rise in identity theft and scams. We should use current accounts for day-to-day spending only. It may be paranoia, but at least there is a line of defence to keep our hard-earned retirement funds safe.

CHAPTER 10

BUSINESS: IT'S TIME TO SELL

QUICK READ

If you run a business, this chapter is for you.

It takes a special person to own and run a business. A person who has spirit to take calculated risks. The reward from those risks is to create vision and something of value. Profit is a powerful motivator, too. But while running a business will be rewarding, it is also stressful. A business demands relentless effort, risking health. Burnout leads to high blood pressure and cholesterol. Thus, before our retirement is hijacked by ill health, we must be prepared to let go. Step back from decades of devotion and enjoy our third age.

A guide to successful retirement

To maximise your business's worth, prepare early for the sale. Shape the business to attract good buyers. See your business as thriving, customers are paying, staff are content, and there is a separation between you and the business. When to tell staff is also important. Announcing the sale too soon can cause anxiety, leading to the loss of skilled personnel. Focus on them before introducing any buyer.

Using a broker is recommended. A broker will keep the sale hidden until you are ready to reveal the sale. They can also act as a buffer if the process becomes frustrating. A sale process will rarely go smoothly.

What your business is worth will be influenced by several factors. While you have emotional attachments, you hope your years of hard work will attract a high price. But a buyer will only pay what they think it's worth. Bridging the gap is the art of negotiation. The key to a balanced negotiation is finding the right price for both parties.

(End of quick read)

CRAFTING YOUR SALE

Running a business requires long hours and strain. And someday these aspects will ambush our health. We feel burned out and exhausted. As a result, we develop high blood pressure and bad cholesterol. Worse still, with age, the number of prescribed medications is growing, and the heart misbehaves.

Although we understand life has limitations, we have a deep connection to our business. Decades have been used to nurture the enterprise. So much so that as we approach the end of working life, we have a fear of letting go. Leaving our business behind is heart-breaking.

While customers have praised your business, if the business name disappears from public fame, few will care. Thus, ask yourself, should you stay working just to preserve the business name? Or, do you reward yourself with retirement life?

The ideal retirement time is when you and the business are both ready. It is time to put away your tools and relish the rewards of retirement. The wrong time is when bad health forces your hand. Selling a business with a sense of urgency is not the ideal time to sell.

In that situation, the sale will become a fire sale. To sell quickly, deep discounting will be used. Your negotiating position is weaker in the sale process. And bargain hunters will gather like birds of prey, making insulting low offers. If you are forced to accept, these vultures make money at your expense.

PREPARING YOURSELF

At the risk of repeating the above, you can prepare yourself by:

- Knowing that life is not eternal.
- Knowing that retirement (from business life) will be challenging.
- Accepting that only a handful of people will care about your departure.
- Accepting that, following the sale, the business is likely to operate with a new name.

Your employees

Over the years, you have formed a good relationship with your loyal and cherished employees. Therefore, when you come to sell, it is natural that you worry about their reaction. You have a sense of concern. Will the buyer look after them?

Although your employees will be sorry to see you go, people rarely stay in a role for over four years. For now, assure them their job is secure as part of the sale process. In a few years, most employees will have moved on. They will find alternative employment elsewhere. Tempted away with offers of promotion and higher wages.

Harsh as it may sound, employees are not your genuine friends. When the time comes, focus on your health and retirement, as you will be mostly forgotten within five years.

Post-business life

After decades of being in charge, be ready for a major mindset shift. Though the desire to "do business" may still be strong, you will notice:

- The telephone will stop ringing.
- Emails will drop away.

- Nobody is demanding your attention.
- The daily adrenaline from stress will evaporate.

Retirement will be an awakening. Within a year, you and your retired status will not concern customers, staff, or suppliers. Your new retirement "business" is to spend time with hobbies and activities to avert the risk of boredom.

PREPARING THE BUSINESS

The earlier you start, the better the asking price. You can shape the business to attract the best offers and thus strengthen your terms at the negotiation table. Depending on the size of your business and management structure, allow a year to get the business ready.

When the time is right and preparations are being made, it is not recommended to tell the staff at the same time. The news of the business being up for sale will make some people anxious. They may take such news badly. And those who do will question their job security and may even leave. Losing experienced staff is the last thing a business needs. Instead, it is time to connect with staff.

Staff

If your staff are on the same journey to grow, improve, and offer the best product or service, your business will have greater value. This is the utopia for all businesses. Because when selling, a buyer sensing low morale, lack of teamwork, or a sea of glum faces will not feel inspired to buy.

Every business is on a journey and the staff on that journey should be on the same bus, metaphorically. And those on the bus should also be in the right seat. A receptionist who is loyal to the company but dislikes dealing with people is not sitting in the right seat.

Encourage them to move to another role. Harsher yet, encourage any employees not on the bus to board or leave.

In an ideal world, your staff should follow your vision. The right people on the bus, sitting in the right seat. But this is the utopia. If you can achieve this and can show that to a buyer, your business should attract a higher price.

Settle any staff disputes before a buyer arrives. Any remaining issues will be declared as part of the sale process.

Happy staff
To make staff happier, increasing pay is not the only answer. This is a short-term pill that will last just for a few paydays. Instead, bring their needs to the fore. Develop a staff review programme focusing on what the business can do for them. It should not be a critical assessment, although you should be free to ask what they see as their weaker skills.

Ask about their ambitions. What training would they like? What do they like and dislike about their job? Can they offer ideas or suggestions to improve the workplace? Many will warm to a review. Staff appreciate having a voice. You may discover that Jacqui on reception has a desire to be a bookkeeper. Feed her the passion.

However, it is important to follow up the review. Give feedback and a plan of action. Failure to do so will dent their loyalty - the review will have no worth to them, and it may even backfire.

Remove any workplace discomfort. Nobody wants to work with rude and angry customers. If left unchecked, employees will feel unhappy and dread coming to work.

The solution is straightforward, but hard. Fire the customer.

Determine all customers should follow the law of the 3P's:
- Polite.
- Pay on time
- Profitable

Allow staff to report rude customers. Consider the merits and then fire the customer if necessary. What would cost you more, losing the customer or losing a skilled staff member? And finally, give them a free holiday for birthdays and special occasions.

Fresh eyes
We all know that first impressions count, and a buyer will have fresh eyes. Does the workplace look chaotic? Is it overflowing with paperwork? A solution here is to introduce a clear desk policy. Before anyone heads home, all desks should be clear and tidy.

Do the decor and fittings look tired? If so, ask the painters to visit. A chance to embrace the company's colours in the workplace.

See flooring, furniture, and equipment with fresh eyes, too. With years of use, wear and tear adds layers of grubbiness. Has anything passed its sell by date?

Review IT and software. It doesn't look good if the business is still using Windows 3.1, Lotus 123, and a yellowing fax machine.

Collecting money
Collect what is owed from late-paying customers and those that fail to pay. A potential buyer will have concerns about any bad debt (which suggests a weak customer or

one that is dissatisfied). Before the buyer arrives, all customers should be paying to terms. You should also resolve any complaints or disputes.

STEPPING BACK

The more a business depends on the owner, the tougher it is to sell. Take, for example, a one-person business. If a business relies on a single individual, after removing their skill and knowledge, there is little else to sell.

The less dependent a business is on its owner, the higher the value. Both in terms of price and how attractive the business is to a potential buyer. Therefore, if the current business structure allows, make yourself dispensable. You should aim to work on the business, not in it.

Think on a grand scale. Divide the business into several departments, such as sales, production, accounts, and administration. If your name is at the head of any department, your goal is to be replaced.

Start by creating an operations manual for each department. Say how you would like that department to be run and how problems are resolved. If your employees are happy and engaged, they are more likely to solve issues without you. Instead, they will refer to your manual.

Then, become a mentor rather than a manager. With more free time, your first holiday in years may be possible.

At first, it is hard. You fear staff will make mistakes and be the ruination of your business. But, if you have happy staff and the right person is sitting in the right seat, errors will be few. Even you make mistakes. Besides, there will come a day when you must let go.

Otherwise, retirement will never bless you.

After making these changes, it is possible that the business will now run and generate income without you.

BE READY TO SELL

The business is now in good shape. Customers are paying to terms, staff are happy, and we are separating ourselves from the business. We have a neat and tidy enterprise to sell.

Your next task is to prepare a teaser. A one-page summary saying what is unique about your business. Something that would spark a buyer's interest.

You could include:
- Your competitive advantage.
- The potential for growth.
- Staff skills and industry knowledge.
- How the geographic location is important.
- Sales and profit margins.

THE BROKER

Using a broker will help you simplify the process, and more importantly, keep the sale confidential. Neither staff, customers, nor local competitors should know. At least in the early stages. A broker will help sell your business anonymously.

Using a broker will have these advantages:
- They have a register of interested clients.
- It improves confidentiality.
- They ensure the buyer has funding.
- They help you with the business valuation.
- They vet potential buyers.
- They suggest terms and conditions of sale.

If negotiations become heated or difficult, a broker can serve as a buffer.

When appointing a broker, ask how they will be paid. They may charge a fee to cover the cost of advertising, but sometimes it is the buyer who pays the broker's commission.

WHAT ACCOUNTS?

Have full accounts covering the last three years ready to review. Full accounts will give the buyer a detailed profit and loss account and a balance sheet.

Profit and loss account

The profit and loss account will reveal the substance of the business. Including how much revenue it generates, the costs, and its profits. The amount of profit is a buyer's first judgement. And how some of your costs compare to income. If staff costs are high (when compared with revenue), they will ask questions. Are there too many employees or not enough revenue?

Buyers will ask whether the owner is working in the business for free. And whether the owner has the business pay for private expenses. This is not to police us. A buyer wants to see a natural profit statement.

A buyer may also ask for the EBITDA. Pronounced, E-BIT-DA, this statement expresses:
Earnings
Before
Interest
Tax
Depreciation
Amortisation.

The EBITDA helps buyers to compare the core potential of different businesses in the same industry. If this seems a little daunting, ask your accountant. For them, it is quick and simple to prepare.

Balance sheet
A balance sheet will show the worth of your business. The worth of your business is the value of the things you own (assets), less the money that is owed (liabilities). A business is said to be solvent when the value of assets is greater. Assets will include the value of equipment, stock, and money in the bank. Liabilities are bank loans, taxes, and money owed to your suppliers.

NON-DISCLOSURE AGREEMENTS
The broker has found a buyer who is eager to learn more. However, before opening the doors to strangers, you must protect yourself from commercial spying. Buyers are not always genuine. Their actual intent may be to look for insider knowledge and headhunt skilled employees. They may have no intention of buying.

To counter this possibility, buyers should be asked to sign an NDA (a non-disclosure agreement). A broker may offer help with the creation of an NDA; it is a legal document to protect the business. If the buyer is genuine, they will be happy to sign.

The NDA will say:
- The parties to the agreement.
- What information has protection, excluding any information already in the public domain?
- The obligations on the buyer to prevent careless release of information.
- What happens to the information if the buyer withdraws? The NDA may request any documents to be returned, destroyed, or deleted.

- Restriction on buyer's ability to recruit employees should the sale not complete.

The NDA may also specify what information you can request from the buyer.

INFORMING STAFF

Finding a broker and telling staff at the same time is being too hasty. This would invite a prolonged period of uncertainty, leading to some staff to seek employment elsewhere. Losing experienced staff is the last thing you need as the buyer reviews your business.

If you wait until the buyer appears in reception, however, this is too late. There will be disbelief and anger. Your staff's loyalty will be put to the test.

The ideal time to announce the sale is just after the buyer signs the NDA. However, before then, rumours may circulate. To counter these rumours, say the business is looking for investment. While this has an element of truth, it should avoid emotive disruptions.

Telling your staff about the sale needs an element of courage. How they will react is part of this moment. And yet woven in between are your words of retirement. It is a defining moment. Once announced, your retirement journey has truly started.

As you reveal the sale, build eagerness for the change. A new owner will bring new opportunities and career progression. Which is likely when a business is being absorbed into something much larger.

INFORMING CUSTOMERS

Never tell your customers that you are selling your business. Your customers are not chattel for you to sell.

If treated this way, many will take offence. Instead, tell them why a new owner is good for the business and how it will benefit them.

Communication and assurances are key to a successful transition. Use all channels of communication to tell the customer. Some will be happy with an e-mail or text, but others need a letter. Most of all, thank the customer for their loyalty over the years and say how you have valued their custom.

THINGS TO HAVE READY
As the sale advances, the buyer will request a stream of information. Which you are happy to provide. However, it can be frustrating at times. The buyer will make a request for information already provided. They ask what seem to you trivial questions. They make pointless demands.

Calm your frustrations by having the following ready:
- The property lease agreement.
- Evidence of statutory compliance (see below).
- Staff employment contracts.
- Staff annual reviews.
- Supplier and service contracts.
- Operational and software licences.

Statutory compliance
The common statutory obligations are:
- Fire safety policy and the named officer.
- Health & safety policy, with a named first aider
- Compliance with the General Data Protection Regulation (GDPR) with a named data controller.
- Compliance with money laundering regulations.
- Current employers' liability insurance.
- PAT testing has declared all electrical equipment safe.

AFTER THE SALE

All parties have signed the agreement, the funds are ready to be transferred. You are at the doorstep of retirement and your dream of a nine-month world cruise beckons.

While a long holiday is tempting, walking away too soon would be reckless. Many agreements will have specific clauses to protect the buyer. They will not pay all the funds until they have the assurance of receiving what the seller has described. Therefore, your new role after the sale is to make sure the buyer is happy.

As you hand over the business, stay with the buyer as a consultant. While this may delay your retirement, this arrangement is ideal for both you and the buyer. This is especially true for service industries where the customer may be resistant to change. If you stay visible as the buyer eases in, the potential loss of business will be reduced.

WHAT'S MY BUSINESS WORTH?

A business is only worth what someone is willing to pay. A disappointing answer for sure, but there are a few ways you can value your enterprise. But the worth of a business has many colours of calculation.

Annual profits

A business can be valued by using the profit average. A multiple is then applied to the average. This is a simple valuation. For example, imagine income for the years to:

31 December 2021 of £50,000
31 December 2022 of £60,000
31 December 2023 of £40,000

The average profit is, therefore, £50,000 per year. The accountant recommends a value of £200,000 - a multiple of four times the average. If the profits stay at this average, it will take four years for the buyer to recover their investment.

Buyer's considerations
- After a review, the buyer may be concerned that profits have fallen to £40,000. They have therefore countered the original valuation with a multiple of three. They are prepared to pay £150,000.
- The buyer also understands that only one person runs the business. Fearing customers will evaporate as the owner leaves, profits may fall again. Therefore, they seek to reduce the offer. For the buyer, there is a risk they will invest in a declining business.

Seller's considerations
The accountant has factored the following into the valuation:
- Geographic advantage
- The high quality of staff or specialist knowledge.
- Strong brand recognition.

As their business is a good match with the buyer's operation, they have spotted high growth opportunity for the buyer. A premium is added to reflect this.

Other factors that can increase valuation are:
- Competition between serious buyers.
- Using the latest software or equipment.
- Owning patents or having technical advantage.

Goodwill
There are parts of a business that have value, but no physical substance - for example, brand reputation and

customer loyalty. We know this as goodwill. A value given to a non-physical asset.

In the example above, the business has (say) physical stock and assets of £150,000, and yet the seller is asking for £200,000. The extra £50,000 represents the brand of the business. However, the value of goodwill is subjective. The value we attach to goodwill will always be what the buyer is prepared to pay.

Value

The value of any business will be driven by the market, not personal expectations. For the seller, there is hope that their years of hard work, heart and soul, will be reflected in the price. Usually because a seller has emotional attachments. The buyer, however, will see things in a colder light. If the expectation gap is too big, there will be an art to finding the right price.

SPEED

The speed of a sale will increase if there is more than one interested party. The faster you can sell, the greater the chances of completion. We also find the final asking price is higher.

On the other hand, a single buyer will hold greater control. They will drive the speed and the terms, sometimes making unreasonable offers. Deadlock may follow and the sale aborted.

The seller can also wipe away negotiations by being too tough. If you take a hard-line, you can harm negotiations. If you have a line beyond which you will not negotiate, a sale can stall. If you become too belligerent in the meeting room, the buyer has the final say. They can walk away.

TYPES OF SALE

There are two main types of agreement. An asset sale or a share sale. An asset sale is where the buyer agrees to buy all, or some of, the assets (and liabilities) of the business. A share sale is where the buyer gains the share capital of the company. The business will continue as normal (in the short term).

Remember to plan your own retirement, too

Planning for and managing the sale of your business will take up a lot of time and energy. But don't forget to keep an eye on your own plans, too – make sure you have a clear plan not just to sell the business but also to make the personal transition into retirement.

AUTHOR'S NOTES

I wrote this book after my research before the big day. Two years before I retired, I was asking myself the same big questions you are asking now. What can I expect during my remaining months at work? What lies ahead after the big day? What will my days become? How will this expanded time be filled? And, it was dawning on me, I was also getting older.

There are some frustrations in life. One of those is when we reach the end of our career. There are few who teach the way of retirement and so I sought the experience of others. And then I read (and read) many books. I did this to gain answers to the big retirement questions.

Feeling ready, I retired in December 2019 with a head full of knowledge. Insightful knowledge that was ripe to help others also thinking about making the big leap into retirement. So, over the last three years I have written this book in the genuine hope that it inspires a way to see your retirement.

LAST DAY OF WORK

On reflection, I would say my last day was a bittersweet day.

I was happy because it was my final plod of familiar commuting. No more hunting for the last parking space at the station. Or having to stand on the overcrowded train, despite the cold early hour. After today, there would be no more pointless meetings and thankless clients. However, it marked the end of familiar faces. The faces I had shared much laughter with every day. This was one of the sadder parts of retirement, leaving these friends behind.

And here was a scary thought. After today I would lose the monthly wage. After forty years of ambition and career building, the safety net of earning and saving would change. Starting tomorrow, my pension became the sole source of income. The same monthly pay to the end of my days.

As a morning person, I usually reached the office first. I unlocked and entered. We had an open-plan office with desks, computers, phones, and seating for around twenty people. As expected, the room was empty; the air was dark, silent, and chilly. An empty room ready for the day.

I flicked on the lights. So far, a normal start to the day. It felt like a birthday, a day to share with friends at work. I did not want any fuss, but would there be anything to mark the occasion? And yes, to my delight, they had remembered. On this my last day, my desk and the space above it were nicely decorated with banners and balloons. On these, I read congratulations and happy retirement.

The last two words hold uniqueness. Not only do they capture a defining moment in life but being wished a happy retirement felt premature. At sixty-four, I was still fit and healthy. Was I cheating on society's norms by not sporting grey hair or being worn out?

The day passed by quickly and as I tied up the last of my loose ends, conversations with co-workers drifted towards my plans for the days to come. Before I knew it, I was standing to give a little speech. I reflected on my time with the company and the good people that I had known for many years.

My manager joined in, too, presented the company's heart-felt good wishes, a card, and a bottle of vintage whisky to sip and savour at leisure. The whisky was named Scallywag. Matured in sherry casks with waves of thick velvety chocolate. There was, however, one observation that surprised me. As I stood with my manager, I noted a few of my co-workers were uninterested. They continued their work as if normality surrounded them.

As the day ended, I packed my remaining belongings and said goodbye to my desk, phone, and computer. I left for the last time, knowing I had represented the company well. And yet, I could not believe this day, that once had seemed decades away, was now behind me. I had adventures and possibilities ahead, but I would miss my coworkers. We had some great times together, both inside and outside the workplace. Would I miss the structure and daily routine? Well, maybe.

After this day, I would have a new life with the luxury of time. Finally, it was time to unwind and enjoy those forgotten hobbies. I knew also that retirement would give me extra time to care for myself. The badges of youth were dropping away.

Every year my weight increased by the smallest of amounts. The blood pressure was not happy, and the doctor was suggesting statins to keep the cholesterol down. However, none of us can stay youthful forever. Retirement naturally leads to thoughts about mortality and the remaining years. If the body or mind declines, retirement life is affected.

MY FIRST DAY OF RETIREMENT

The day started as usual. Today was Monday and my wonderful wife (being younger than me) was still working. Thus, on this Monday morning we woke at the usual time of 5.30 am. Such are the pleasures of walking our two dogs.

Dogs walked in the dark, along muddy paths, I was now home. Showered and dressed, I was ready for the communal battle to work. Except today, on this very first occasion, I was in casual attire. Today the car was staying on the driveway. The station car park had one extra space, and the train was a passenger lighter. I was at home. On a workday!

I felt exceptionally odd. As if I was "pulling a sickie", ditching the boss for extra duvet time in a warm bed. But I was not sick, or poorly, or otherwise. I was staying at home for the best of reasons. There was no need to fear the boss's interrogation tomorrow. There were no deadlines to meet, no need to meet thankless clients. I was free to do as I pleased. This day was wholly mine.

A little later I bought a newspaper. A short walk to the supermarket secured a bread roll and some bacon. Not my usual breakfast but, having the time to cook, it seemed the right thing to do. However, even with lashings of tomato sauce, the eating proved a rather grim disappointment.

As the morning sky was clear and the air warm, I sat in the garden with my fresh newspaper. Turning the pages, I had time to *read* rather than scan the headlines. This, I thought, is surely the retirement life.

A guide to successful retirement

Later that morning, I met a friend who had retired a week earlier. We skipped our usual pint at the George and Dragon because of the early hour. Instead, we sat in the park, sipping cafe coffee. For the first time I glimpsed life beyond the walls of work. Park activity that was once unseen now surrounded me. And we sat in conversation for a while. We agreed how lucky we were to have this alternative non-working lifestyle. With good health and twenty years ahead, we could pursue hobbies and passions.

Before today, I had pondered upon those hobbies I had enjoyed as a young boy. Wooden aircraft models were one of my early passions and, in retirement, I was going to make that latent passion my new art. I also wanted to make a bird table. Another of my childhood passions - watching the garden birds. And thus, I raided the shed for some wood and began sawing, banging nails, and painting.

Today, I achieved something I seldom do. I discovered one surprising thing about retirement. Having plenty of time allows me to savour activities without the background hum of being rushed. There was no need to squeeze hobbies into the weekend anymore. After this first day, all time was now my own.

www.ingramcontent.com/pod-product-compliance
Lightning Source LLC
Chambersburg PA
CBHW071955260326
41914CB00004B/810

* 9 7 8 1 0 6 8 6 4 1 5 2 7 *